Katie –
To the best little "cooker"

XX OO
Mom + Dad

We love you so much!!

A CELEBRATION OF

HEARTLAND RECIPES

Dining Dakota Style

FROM THE

JUNIOR LEAGUE OF

SIOUX FALLS

A CELEBRATION OF

HEARTLAND RECIPES

Dining Dakota Style

FROM THE

JUNIOR LEAGUE OF

SIOUX FALLS

A CELEBRATION OF
HEARTLAND RECIPES

Dining Dakota Style

FROM THE
JUNIOR LEAGUE OF
SIOUX FALLS

Published by the Junior League of Sioux
Falls, Inc.

Copyright © 2004 by
The Junior League of Sioux Falls, Inc.
3101 West 41st Street
Suite 208
Sioux Falls, South Dakota 57105
605-336-9469
www.jlsiouxfalls.org

This cookbook is a collection of favorite
recipes, which are not necessarily original
recipes. The cookbook development
committee researched and wrote the
non-recipe text as accurately as possible.

Library of Congress Control
Number: 2003104333
ISBN: 0-9729313-0-9

Edited, Designed, and Manufactured
by Favorite Recipes® Press
an Imprint of

P.O. Box 305142
Nashville, Tennessee 37230
800-358-0560

Art Director: Steve Newman
Book Design: David Malone
Project Manager: Tanis Westbrook

Manufactured in the
United States of America
First Printing: 2004 - 10,000 copies

On the cover:
Falls on the Big Sioux River at Falls Park
Dining set:
Ethan Allen Home Interiors
Floral design:
Josephine's Unique Floral Designery
Tableware:
Larsen Designs Limited
Photographer:
Greg Latza,
Peoplescapes Publishing

Cookbook Committee

DEVELOPMENT COMMITTEE

Melissa Anderson	Development Chair	Jennifer Larson
Emily Bartels	Amy Trankle Kusmak	Shelley Pate
Danylle Hampton		Jeni Thomas
Beverly Harvey		Suzanne Toll
		Shelly Voecks

MARKETING COMMITTEE

Nadine Amundson	Marketing Chairs	Cathy Krueger
Jennifer Edwards	Amy Olson	Lynda Pfeifle
	Angi Gulbranson	Suzanne Veenis

Special Thanks

The development and marketing committees would like to extend a

SPECIAL THANKS

to those who helped in the creation and development of

photography, non-recipe text,

wholesale accounts, and cookbook partnerships.

Shirley Cink	Jane Nutter Johnson	Nancy Olsen
Lisa Davis	Mark Kayser	Kristen Peterson
Leslie Elliott	Greg Latza	Dana Sandene
Jayne Erickson	Kathy Luke	Sarah Sharp
Monica Fehrs	Pam Nelson	Johnny Sundby
Kyle Greenfield		Laura Wicks

Contributors

The Junior League of Sioux Falls would like to
offer special thanks to our major contributors for
their gracious support of *Dining Dakota Style*.

COOKBOOK PARTNERS

Avera McKennan Hospital

The Everist Company

Sioux Valley Hospital

Wells Fargo

The Next Stage®

PROMOTIONAL PARTNERS

HenkinSchultz Communication Arts

KSFY Television

Midcontinent Communications

Midcontinent Radio (KELO-FM)

CHAPTER PARTNERS

First National Bank

Heart Hospital of South Dakota

Home Federal Bank

Howalt-McDowell Insurance Incorporated

Mahlander's Appliance and Lighting

Preface

OUR MISSION

The Junior League of Sioux Falls is an organization of women committed to promoting voluntarism, developing the potential of women, and improving communities through the effective action and leadership of trained volunteers. Its purpose is exclusively educational and charitable.

The Junior League of Sioux Falls reaches out to women of all races, religions, and national origins who demonstrate an interest in and commitment to voluntarism.

OUR COMMUNITY COMMITMENT

The Junior League of Sioux Falls, originally established as the Junior Service League, was formed in 1978 and was accepted into the Association of Junior Leagues International, Inc., in 1985. Since that time, members have raised more than $235,000 for the Sioux Falls area. Each year, our members contribute more than 5,000 hours of volunteer service.

Through the vision and dedication of its members, the Junior League of Sioux Falls works to provide family support, focusing on the needs of children and their parents. Some of the League's current and past projects include the Rolling Readers Program, the Children's Studio at the Washington Pavilion of Arts and Sciences, Refugee and Immigrant Women's Network, Habitat for Humanity House, Children's Medical Library, CASA Program, Ronald McDonald House, Mentor Moms, Race for the Cure®, and Done-in-a-Day projects.

OUR COOKBOOK PROJECT

Research for *Dining Dakota Style* began in the year 2000. League members voted to produce a cookbook in the fall of 2001, with proceeds going to benefit the community of Sioux Falls and the charitable activities of our organization. League members, their families, friends, and neighbors submitted hundreds of recipes, participated in numerous tasting parties, and voted on their favorite dishes. In addition, the cookbook committee collaborated in the design and development of the book, which included all writing, photography selection, and chapter organization. As a result, *Dining Dakota Style* was created. We hope you enjoy this delightful cuisine as you sample the picturesque beauty of our state and experience dining Dakota style!

MAYOR DAVE MUNSON
CITY OF SIOUX FALLS

224 West Ninth Street • Sioux Falls, SD • 57104-6407
(605) 367-7200 • (605) 367-8490 FAX • (605) 367-7039 Hearing Impaired
Web site: www.siouxfalls.org

March 2003

Greetings!

As Mayor of the City of Sioux Falls, I am pleased and honored to endorse *Dining Dakota Style*, the official cookbook of Sioux Falls. This cookbook is a wonderful collection of tried-and-true recipes, photographs, and information about Sioux Falls and of the State of South Dakota.

Your purchase of the *Dining Dakota Style* cookbook will support the many fine programs endorsed by the Junior League of Sioux Falls through their generous volunteer efforts.

Thank you for your purchase of this delightful cookbook. "Bon Appetit!"

Sincerely,

Dave Munson
Mayor

Table of Contents

Heartland Beginnings

Harvest Grains

City Lights

Main Carvings

Table of Contents

Introduction

Welcome to *Dining Dakota Style*. Join us as we explore the rich heritage of South Dakota through the treasured recipes shared in this cookbook. Our state is home to the beautiful, gold-lined Black Hills, the stunning Badlands, the magnificent carvings of Mount Rushmore National Memorial and Crazy Horse Memorial, wide open prairies, and many tributaries of the Missouri River, including the Big Sioux River. Named for the early inhabitants of our state, the great Sioux Nation of Indians, the Sioux River gives rise to the majestic Sioux Falls pictured on our cover and the namesake of our city.

The desire for land and a new life brought the first European settlers to the Dakota Territory in the mid 1800s. These pioneers brought with them the flavors of their native lands of Germany, Russia, Ireland, and Scandinavia. Their influences can still be found today in the culture and lifestyle of the people of South Dakota.

With great pride, we share this array of tastes that range from traditional to contemporary. *Dining Dakota Style* offers diverse cuisine and takes you on a breathtaking photographic journey through our state. May you experience the warmth and hospitality found in South Dakota as you prepare these recipes for your family and friends.

Springtime Brunch

As gardeners eagerly prepare their flowerbeds and vegetable
gardens, celebrate spring's arrival by serving this special brunch.

Brandy Slush

Frozen Fruit Cups

Sausage Soufflé

Blueberry Lattice Coffee Cake

Book Club Luncheon

Serve this light meal at your next gathering to discuss
the latest on the best-seller list.

Creamy Chocolate-Dipped Strawberries

Tomato Bisque

Wild Rice and Chicken Salad

Carrot Rolls with Garlic and Herb Spread

Lemon Buttermilk Loaves

School Night Supper

For families on the go, this meal means less time spent in
the kitchen and more time spent with loved ones.

Apple Snicker Salad

Overnight Chicken Bake

Creole Corn

Chocolate Butterfinger Cookies

Midsummer Night Dinner

End a perfect summer day by firing up the grill
and entertaining guests on the deck.

Perfect Lady

Wild Turkey Kabobs

Mediterranean Pasta Salad

Party Bread

Frozen Berry Dessert

An Elegant Evening

Dazzle your friends and family with this spectacular meal
as part of an enchanted evening.

Baked Herb Havarti Cheese

Roquefort Waldorf Salad on Mixed Greens

Royal Beef Tenderloin

Parmesan Smashed Potatoes

Spinach-Stuffed Portobellos

Molten Chocolate Cakes

Fall Family Gathering

Take pleasure in all that autumn has to offer by picking apples at the orchard,
searching for the best pumpkin in the patch, and gathering around the table with family.

Crostini with Dried Tomato and Feta Spread

Fresh Cranberry Salad

Pecan Chicken

Asparagus Bake

Grandma's Rolls

Chocolate Truffle Cheesecake

After the Hunt

Savor the unique flavors of this meal brought
to you from nature to the table.

Midwest Pâté

Broccoli Raisin Salad

Pheasant Pierre

Roasted Cauliflower

Oregano and Cheese Bread

Chocolate Raspberry Cake

Cozy Winter Dinner

When powdery snow covers the ground and ice glistens on the trees outside,
spend an evening basking in the warmth of the fire, enjoying this hearty winter meal.

Wassail

Layered Pesto and Tomato Torta

Winter Pear Salad

Creamy Wild Rice Soup

Cracklin' Pork

Cheese Scalloped Carrots

Apple Cake with Caramel Sauce

Party Fare

Create a bit of history and set the tone for a memorable event
when you serve these festive dishes at your next party.

Sweet Chile-Glazed Chicken Wings

Smoked Salmon and Boursin Canapés

Stuffed French Bread

Beef Tenderloin with Caper Mayonnaise on Baguettes

Spinach and Feta Strudel

Mile-High New York-Style Cheesecake

Double Chocolate Truffles

Lemon and White Chocolate Shortbread

Heartland Beginnings

Appetizers and Beverages

Badlands National Park • *Johnny Sundby, Dakota Skies Photography*

The Badlands National Park, located in the southwestern portion of our state, is breathtaking in appearance, and its geologic story is equally as colorful and fascinating. These sharply eroded buttes, pinnacles, and spires serve as a window to the past, containing the world's richest fossil beds from the Oligocene epoch, dating 40 to 25 million years ago. These formations are virtual sculptures created by nature through the erosive forces of wind and water. The flat-lying stratification of the landforms adds to the grandeur of the region. The dramatic orange and gray bands of sediment can be traced horizontally from ridge to ridge, across the ravine, binding together individual parts of this ever-changing scenery.

Just southwest of the Badlands you will find another of South Dakota's archeological treasures, the Mammoth Site, located near Hot Springs, South Dakota. Here, 26,000 years ago, Columbian mammoths became trapped in a 65-foot sinkhole. These fossils were preserved intact and undetected until 1974, when a local developer began construction on a housing project and happened upon this incredible discovery. The Mammoth Site offers visitors an opportunity to view current excavations and experience hands-on exhibits in the museum.

South Dakota's prehistoric elements provide unique opportunities to peer back in time. With the recipes in this chapter, you too will create a bit of history. Whether used as a prelude to a special meal or as the highlight of a festive cocktail party, these tantalizing appetizers and beverages will set the tone for a memorable event.

Layered Pesto and Tomato Torta

24 ounces light cream cheese, softened
1/4 cup (1/2 stick) margarine or butter, softened
3 tablespoons milk
1/2 teaspoon white pepper
1 (7-ounce) container pesto, drained
2 tablespoons Italian bread crumbs
1 (8-ounce) jar marinated sun-dried tomatoes,
    drained and finely chopped
Fresh parsley, chopped

Combine the cream cheese, margarine, milk and white pepper in a mixing bowl and beat until blended. Spread 1 cup of the mixture over the bottom of a foil-lined 4×8-inch dish. Combine the pesto and bread crumbs in a bowl and mix well. Spread the pesto mixture over the cream cheese layer. Spread 1 cup of the cream cheese mixture over the pesto layer. Sprinkle with the sun-dried tomatoes. Spread the remaining 1 cup cream cheese mixture over the sun-dried tomatoes. Chill, covered, for 4 to 8 hours. Invert onto a serving plate. Sprinkle with the parsley. Serve with bread rounds or crackers.

Serves 18 to 24

HINT—For a festive holiday look, shape the cream cheese mixture into a pyramid. Smooth the sides with a knife, and freeze for 20 minutes. Cut the pyramid horizontally into thirds. Layer pesto and sun-dried tomatoes between each layer. Chill, covered, until firm. Place a small ornament on top for decoration.

Chicken and Chile Cheesecake

2 teaspoons chicken bouillon granules
1 tablespoon hot water
24 ounces cream cheese, softened
1 1/2 teaspoons chili powder
1/2 to 1 teaspoon hot sauce
2 eggs
1 to 2 cups finely chopped cooked chicken
1 (4-ounce) can chopped green chiles, drained
Shredded Cheddar cheese
Sliced green onions (optional)

Dissolve the bouillon granules in the water in a small bowl. Beat the cream cheese at high speed in a mixing bowl until light and fluffy. Add the chili powder and hot sauce and beat until blended. Add the eggs 1 at a time, beating well after each addition. Stir in the bouillon mixture, chicken and green chiles.

Spoon the mixture into a lightly greased 9-inch springform pan. Bake at 300 degrees for 45 minutes. Turn off the oven. Let the cheesecake stand in the oven, leaving the door partially open, for 1 hour. Remove the cheesecake from the oven and let stand for 15 minutes.

Place the cheesecake on a serving plate. Remove the side of the pan. Top the cheesecake with Cheddar cheese and green onions. Serve warm with tortilla chips.

Serves 16

HINT—This savory cheesecake requires no fussy assembly like individual appetizers and makes an excellent choice for larger parties. This makes a beautiful presentation when served on a pedestal plate.

Crostini with Dried Tomato and Feta Spread

1 (3-ounce) jar oil-packed sun-dried tomatoes
1 (8-ounce) loaf French bread
1/4 cup chopped onion
1 teaspoon capers
1 garlic clove, minced
3 ounces cream cheese, softened
2 tablespoons milk
1 cup (4 ounces) crumbled feta cheese

Drain the sun-dried tomatoes, reserving the oil. Finely chop the sun-dried tomatoes. Cut the bread on the diagonal into 20 slices. Arrange the bread slices on a baking sheet. Brush 1 side of each bread slice with the reserved oil. Bake at 400 degrees for 8 minutes or until the bread is light brown, turning once halfway through the baking time.

Combine the sun-dried tomatoes, onion, capers and garlic in a bowl and mix well. Beat the cream cheese and milk in a mixing bowl until blended. Stir in the feta cheese.

Spread the cheese mixture on the oiled side of the toasted bread. Top with the sun-dried tomato mixture.

Makes 20 crostini

Peppered Cheese Ball

24 ounces cream cheese, softened
1/2 cup (1 stick) butter, softened
1/2 cup (2 ounces) freshly grated Parmesan cheese
1 package ranch salad dressing mix
Coarsely ground pepper

Combine the cream cheese, butter, Parmesan cheese and salad dressing mix in a food processor and process until smooth. Shape into balls. Grease 2 or 3 small plastic food storage containers. Sprinkle pepper liberally over the sides and bottoms of the prepared containers. Place the cheese balls in the prepared containers. Chill until ready to serve. To serve, remove from the containers and sprinkle with additional pepper. Serve with pretzels.

Makes 2 or 3 cheese balls

Baked Herb Havarti Cheese

2 tablespoons Dijon mustard
12 ounces Havarti cheese
1 tablespoon chopped fresh dill weed
1 tablespoon parsley
1 teaspoon chopped fresh basil
1 teaspoon fennel seeds
1 sheet frozen puff pastry, thawed
1 egg, beaten

Spread the Dijon mustard over the cheese. Sprinkle with the dill weed, parsley, basil and fennel seeds. Place the cheese in the center of the pastry sheet. Fold the sides to overlap at the center, trimming the excess pastry and pressing the edges to seal.

Place the prepared cheese seam side down on a plate. Chill, covered, for 30 minutes to 10 hours. Place the cheese on a greased baking sheet.

Bake at 375 degrees for 20 minutes. Brush with the egg. Bake for 10 minutes longer. Let stand for 5 minutes. Serve with sliced pears, apples or crackers.

Serves 12 to 15

Mushroom Pâté

$1/2$ cup finely chopped green onions with tops
2 tablespoons butter
1 cup finely chopped mushrooms
1 tablespoon lemon juice
$1/8$ teaspoon cayenne pepper
Salt to taste
Black pepper to taste
2 tablespoons chopped fresh dill weed
$1/3$ cup sour cream

Sauté the green onions in the butter in a skillet for 1 minute. Add the mushrooms, lemon juice, cayenne pepper, salt and black pepper. Cook for 4 minutes, stirring occasionally. Remove from the heat. Stir in the dill weed and sour cream. Serve with toast points or crackers. You may substitute $1/2$ teaspoon dried dill weed for the fresh dill weed.

Serves 2 to 4

Black Bean Salsa

1/4 cup olive oil
1/4 cup red wine vinegar
1/2 to 1 teaspoon cayenne pepper
2 (15-ounce) cans black beans, drained and rinsed
11/4 cups fresh or frozen corn kernels
1 pound tomatoes, chopped
1 bunch green onions, chopped
1 green bell pepper, finely chopped
1 red bell pepper, finely chopped

Whisk together the olive oil, vinegar and cayenne pepper in a bowl. Combine the black beans, corn, tomatoes, green onions and bell peppers in a large bowl and mix well. Add the vinegar mixture and mix well. Serve with tortilla chips.

Serves 18 to 20

HINT—For fun homemade tortilla chips, cut flour tortillas into star shapes using a cookie cutter. Sprinkle the tortillas with chili powder. Bake at 350 degrees for 8 to 10 minutes.

Sun-Dried Tomato Dip

1/4 cup oil-packed sun-dried tomatoes, drained and chopped
8 ounces cream cheese, softened
1/2 cup mayonnaise
1/4 cup sour cream
10 dashes of Tabasco sauce
1 teaspoon kosher salt
3/4 teaspoon pepper
2 scallions, thinly sliced

Combine the sun-dried tomatoes, cream cheese, mayonnaise, sour cream, Tabasco sauce, salt and pepper in a food processor and process until smooth. Add the scallions and pulse 2 times. Spoon into a serving dish. Serve with crackers, tortilla chips or vegetables.

Serves 15

Cheese Straws

8 ounces sharp Cheddar cheese, shredded and softened
1/2 cup (1 stick) butter, softened
1 teaspoon sugar
3/4 teaspoon salt
3/4 teaspoon cayenne pepper, or to taste
1 1/4 cups flour

Combine the cheese and butter in a mixing bowl and beat until smooth. Add the sugar, salt and cayenne pepper and mix well. Add the flour 1/2 at a time, mixing well after each addition.

Place the dough in a cookie press or pastry bag fitted with a star tip. Press into 3- or 4-inch-long straws onto a baking sheet.

Bake at 350 degrees for 8 to 10 minutes or just until the edges begin to brown. Cool on a wire rack. You may freeze the cheese straws until ready to serve.

Makes 80 cheese straws

Beef Tenderloin with Caper Mayonnaise

24 (1/4- to 1/2-inch-thick) baguette slices
2 tablespoons olive oil
1/2 cup mayonnaise
1/4 cup (1 ounce) grated Parmesan
   cheese
2 tablespoons chopped fresh chives

2 to 4 tablespoons capers
1/4 teaspoon garlic powder
1/2 pound cooked beef tenderloin,
   thinly sliced
2 Italian plum tomatoes, thinly sliced

Arrange the baguette slices on an ungreased baking sheet. Brush with the olive oil. Bake at 350 degrees for 8 to 10 minutes or until crisp. Let cool for 5 minutes.

Combine the mayonnaise, cheese, chives, capers and garlic powder in a bowl and mix well. Spread the mayonnaise mixture on the baguette slices. Top with the beef tenderloin and tomatoes. Garnish with chives. You may substitute thinly sliced roast beef for the beef tenderloin.

Serves 10 to 12

Chicken and Mushroom Bites

2 pounds chicken breasts, cooked and
   chopped
1/3 cup chopped onion
2 (8-ounce) cans water chestnuts,
   drained
1 (4-ounce) can mushrooms, drained
1/4 cup flour
1 teaspoon salt

1/2 teaspoon garlic powder
1/4 teaspoon black pepper
Dash of cayenne pepper
1/4 cup soy sauce
2 tablespoons sherry
2 tablespoons Worcestershire sauce
3 egg whites, stiffly beaten
Vegetable oil for frying

Combine the chicken, onion, water chestnuts and mushrooms in a bowl. Chop the mixture in batches in a food processor. Spoon the mixture into a large bowl. Add the flour, salt, garlic powder, black pepper, cayenne pepper, soy sauce, sherry, Worcestershire sauce and egg whites and mix well.

Shape by teaspoonfuls into balls. Brown on all sides in hot oil in a skillet; drain. Serve warm. These may be made ahead of time and frozen. To serve, bake at 350 degrees for 10 to 15 minutes or until heated through.

Makes 60 bites

Sweet Chili-Glazed Chicken Wings

1/4 cup olive oil

3 tablespoons soy sauce

3 tablespoons chopped fresh cilantro

2 tablespoons minced garlic

2 tablespoons minced fresh gingerroot

1/2 teaspoon red pepper flakes

2 pounds chicken wings

1 cup rice wine vinegar

1/2 cup water

1/2 cup packed brown sugar

1 tablespoon chili garlic sauce

Combine the olive oil, soy sauce, cilantro, garlic, gingerroot and red pepper flakes in a bowl and mix well. Add the chicken wings and toss to coat. Marinate in the refrigerator for 2 to 12 hours; drain. Arrange the chicken wings on a baking sheet. Bake at 400 degrees for 20 minutes.

Combine the vinegar, water, brown sugar and chili garlic sauce in a small saucepan. Cook for 20 minutes, stirring frequently. Pour the sauce over the chicken wings. Serve immediately.

Serves 8 to 10

Stuffed Mushrooms

16 ounces large fresh mushrooms

1 cup (2 sticks) butter

1 cup minced onion

3 or 4 garlic cloves, minced

1/4 cup chopped parsley

1 1/2 teaspoons salt

1/2 teaspoon oregano

1 cup dry bread crumbs

1/2 cup (2 ounces) grated Parmesan
    cheese

Remove the stems from the mushroom caps. Dice the stems. Melt the butter in a skillet over medium heat. Sauté the diced mushroom stems, onion, garlic, parsley, salt and oregano for 5 minutes or until the onion is tender. Stir in the bread crumbs and cheese. Remove from the heat. Spoon the mixture into the mushroom caps. Arrange the stuffed mushrooms stuffed side up on a baking sheet. Broil 5 to 6 inches from the heat source for 8 to 10 minutes or until the mushrooms are tender. Serve immediately.

Serves 8

Crispy Fried Eggplant and Mozzarella Finger Sandwiches

4 Japanese eggplant
6 tablespoons olive oil, divided
Salt to taste
Freshly ground pepper to taste
3 garlic cloves
1/2 cup fresh basil
1/4 cup flat-leaf parsley
1/8 teaspoon red pepper flakes
16 ounces fresh mozzarella cheese, cut into 1/4-inch slices
3 eggs, lightly beaten
1 cup (4 ounces) grated Parmesan cheese
Vegetable oil for frying

Cut the eggplant on the diagonal into 1/2-inch slices. Brush the eggplant with 3 tablespoons of the olive oil. Sprinkle with salt and pepper. Arrange on a baking sheet. Bake at 425 degrees for 15 minutes or until golden brown.

Combine the garlic, basil, parsley, red pepper flakes and remaining 3 tablespoons olive oil in a food processor and process until blended. Spread the herb mixture on half the eggplant slices. Top each prepared eggplant slice with a slice of mozzarella cheese and the remaining eggplant slices.

Dip the eggplant sandwiches in the beaten egg. Roll in the Parmesan cheese. Heat 1/2 inch oil in a skillet. Cook the eggplant sandwiches in the hot oil for 2 minutes on each side or until brown; drain. Serve warm.

Makes 20 finger sandwiches

HINT—Choose eggplant that has a glossy shine. Overripe eggplant has a dull color and a bitter taste.

Smoked Salmon and Boursin Canapés

1 French baguette, thinly sliced
8 ounces cream cheese, softened
1/2 cup (1 stick) butter, softened
1 garlic clove, minced
1 teaspoon oregano
1/4 teaspoon basil
1/4 teaspoon dill weed

1/4 teaspoon marjoram
1/4 teaspoon thyme
1/4 teaspoon pepper
Dijon mustard in a squeeze bottle
8 ounces smoked salmon
3 tablespoons capers
Fresh dill weed

Arrange the baguette slices on a baking sheet. Bake at 450 degrees for 6 to 8 minutes or until golden brown. Cool on a wire rack.

Combine the cream cheese, butter, garlic, oregano, basil, 1/4 teaspoon dill weed, marjoram, thyme and pepper in a food processor and process until smooth. Spread the cheese mixture on the toasted baguette slices.

Squeeze a small amount of Dijon mustard onto each baguette slice. Top each slice with 1 to 2 teaspoons of the salmon, 3 capers and a sprig of fresh dill weed.

The cheese mixture may be prepared in advance and stored in the refrigerator for up to 1 week or in the freezer for up to 3 months.

Serves 18

Artichoke Frittata

3 (6-ounce) jars marinated artichoke
    hearts, drained and finely chopped
1 onion, finely chopped
8 ounces sharp Cheddar cheese,
    shredded

4 eggs, lightly beaten
6 soda crackers, finely crushed
1/4 teaspoon salt
1/4 teaspoon pepper
Dash of Tabasco sauce

Combine the artichoke hearts, onion, cheese, eggs, cracker crumbs, salt, pepper and Tabasco sauce in a bowl and mix well. Spoon the mixture into a greased 8-inch square baking dish. Bake at 325 degrees for 1 hour. Let cool slightly. Serve warm or at room temperature.

Serves 12 to 16

Spinach and Feta Strudel

2 pounds fresh spinach with stems, washed
1 1/4 cups (2 1/2 sticks) unsalted butter, divided
1/2 cup minced white parts of green onions
6 ounces feta cheese, crumbled
1/2 cup fresh bread crumbs, divided
4 egg whites
1/2 cup minced fresh parsley
4 tablespoons fresh dill weed, or 2 tablespoons dried dill weed
Salt to taste
Freshly ground pepper to taste
12 sheets frozen phyllo pastry, thawed

Cook the spinach in a small amount of water in a skillet just until wilted. Plunge immediately into cold water to stop the cooking process; drain. Roll the spinach in a clean kitchen towel to absorb the excess moisture. Purée in a food processor.

Melt 1/4 cup of the butter in a small skillet. Sauté the green onions in the melted butter for 5 minutes. Combine green onions, cheese, 2 tablespoons of the bread crumbs, egg whites, parsley, dill weed, salt, pepper and spinach in a bowl and beat until blended. Adjust the seasonings.

Melt the remaining 1 cup butter. Unroll the thawed but still chilled phyllo onto waxed paper set on a damp towel. Keep the unused portion of the dough covered with waxed paper topped with a damp towel to prevent it from drying out while you are working. Place 1 phyllo sheet in front of you lengthwise. Brush the sheet lightly with melted butter. Sprinkle with 1 teaspoon of the bread crumbs. Layer 3 additional phyllo sheets on top, brushing each sheet with butter and sprinkling with bread crumbs. Spread 1/3 of the spinach mixture over the top.

Roll as for a jelly roll. Place the roll on a generously buttered large baking sheet with sides. Repeat the process twice with the remaining phyllo sheets, butter, bread crumbs and spinach mixture. Bake at 375 degrees for 30 to 35 minutes or until golden brown. Cut into 1-inch slices with a serrated knife.

Serves 42

Focaccia

1 (10-ounce) package refrigerator pizza
    dough
2 garlic cloves, pressed
2 cups (8 ounces) shredded mozzarella
    cheese, divided

2/3 cup grated Romano cheese, divided
2 teaspoons oregano, divided
2 plum tomatoes, sliced

Roll the dough into a 12-inch circle on a lightly greased baking sheet or a baking stone. Spread the garlic over the dough. Sprinkle with 1 cup of the mozzarella cheese, 1/3 cup of the Romano cheese and 1 teaspoon of the oregano. Layer the tomatoes over the cheese. Sprinkle with the remaining 1 cup mozzarella cheese, 1/3 cup Romano cheese and 1 teaspoon oregano. Bake at 350 degrees for 30 to 35 minutes or until the crust is golden brown and the cheese is melted.

Serves 8

Stuffed French Bread

1 loaf French bread
2 tablespoons sesame seeds
1/2 cup (1 stick) butter
1 (14-ounce) can artichoke hearts,
    drained and chopped
2 cups (8 ounces) cubed Monterey Jack
    cheese
1 1/2 cups sour cream

3 or 4 garlic cloves, pressed
2 teaspoons lemon pepper
1 cup (4 ounces) shredded Cheddar
    cheese
1 (3-ounce) can black olives, drained
    and sliced
2 tablespoons chopped fresh parsley

Slice the bread in half lengthwise and scoop out the center, tearing the scooped-out bread into chunks. Reserve the bread shells. Sauté the bread chunks and sesame seeds in the melted butter in a skillet until brown. Let cool slightly.

Combine the artichoke hearts, Monterey Jack cheese, sour cream, garlic and lemon pepper in a bowl and mix well. Add the bread mixture and mix well. Spoon the mixture into the reserved bread shells. Sprinkle with the Cheddar cheese.

Bake at 350 degrees for 25 to 30 minutes or until the cheese is melted. Top with the olives. Sprinkle with the parsley. Slice and serve warm.

Serves 9 to 12

Creamy Chocolate-Dipped Strawberries

1 cup (6 ounces) semisweet chocolate chips
1/2 cup (3 ounces) vanilla chips
1 tablespoon shortening
2 pints fresh strawberries, rinsed and patted dry

Combine the chocolate chips, vanilla chips and shortening in a microwave-safe bowl. Microwave on High until the chips are melted, stirring every 15 seconds. Dip the strawberries in the chocolate mixture, covering the bottom 2/3 of each strawberry.

Shake gently to remove excess chocolate. Place on a waxed paper-lined tray. Chill, covered, for 1 hour or until the chocolate coating is set.

Makes about 3 dozen

HINT—Dipped strawberries should be refrigerated just long enough to set the chocolate. Do not store the dipped strawberries in the refrigerator. For 2 pints white chocolate-dipped strawberries, use 1 1/2 cups white chocolate chips.

Pineapple Punch

2 cups water

3 1/2 cups sugar, divided

1 fresh pineapple, peeled, cored and cubed

1/4 cup lemon juice

1 1/4 cups brandy

1 (25-ounce) bottle dry Champagne

1/4 teaspoon cream of tartar

1/3 cup hot water

3 egg whites

Combine 2 cups water and 2 1/2 cups of the sugar in a large saucepan. Boil until the sugar dissolves, stirring constantly. Let stand until cool. Chill, covered, in the refrigerator. Purée the pineapple in a food processor. Combine the sugar mixture, pineapple, lemon juice, brandy and Champagne in an airtight container. Freeze for 8 hours.

Combine the remaining 1 cup sugar, the cream of tartar and 1/3 cup hot water in a heavy saucepan. Cook over medium heat until the sugar dissolves, stirring constantly. Cook over medium heat to 240 degrees on a candy thermometer; do not stir.

Beat the egg whites in a mixing bowl until stiff peaks form. Add the sugar mixture gradually, beating constantly until stiff peaks form. Chill, covered, until needed.

Remove the pineapple mixture from the freezer and let stand for 1 hour. Place in a large punch bowl and stir the mixture with a large metal spoon until slushy. Fold in the egg white mixture. Serve immediately.

Makes 3 quarts

HINT—A gallon of punch fills about 32 punch cups. Expect each guest to drink 2 to 3 cups, so a gallon will serve approximately 12 people.

Lemonade Bourbon Punch

2 (8-ounce) cans frozen lemonade concentrate, thawed
13/4 cups orange juice, chilled
3/4 cup lemon juice, chilled
1 (2-liter) bottle lemon-lime soda, chilled
1 quart club soda, chilled
1 pint bourbon, chilled

Combine the lemonade concentrate, orange juice, lemon juice, lemon-lime soda, club soda and bourbon in a large bowl and mix well. Pour over ice into a large punch bowl.

Makes 18 cups

HINT—To make an ice ring, place desired fruit in a ring-shaped mold. Add just enough water to cover the fruit. Freeze until firm. Fill the remainder of the mold with water and freeze until solid.

Brandy Slush

9 cups water, divided
2 cups sugar
4 tea bags
1 (12-ounce) can frozen orange juice concentrate, thawed
1 (12-ounce) can frozen lemonade concentrate, thawed
2 cups brandy
Lemon-lime soda

Bring 7 cups of the water to a boil in a saucepan. Add the sugar. Cook until the sugar is dissolved, stirring constantly; remove from the heat. Let stand until cool.

Bring the remaining 2 cups water to a boil in a saucepan. Add the tea bags; remove from the heat. Let stand until cool. Discard the tea bags.

Combine the sugar mixture, tea, orange juice concentrate, lemonade concentrate and brandy in a large bowl and mix well. Freeze, covered, until slushy. To serve, spoon into glasses until 2/3 full. Pour lemon-lime soda into each glass to fill.

Serves 20

Vodka Slush

5 cups water
1¹/₂ cups sugar
1 (12-ounce) can frozen lemonade concentrate, thawed
1 (12-ounce) can frozen orange juice concentrate, thawed
2 cups vodka
2 cups pineapple juice
Lemon-lime soda

Bring the water to a boil in a saucepan. Add the sugar. Cook until the sugar dissolves, stirring constantly; remove from the heat. Let stand until cool. Combine the sugar mixture, lemonade concentrate, orange juice concentrate, vodka and pineapple juice in a large bowl and mix well. Freeze, covered, until slushy. To serve, fill glasses ¹/₂ full. Pour lemon-lime soda into the glasses to fill. You may substitute ginger ale for the lemon-lime soda.

Serves 20

Sparkling Cranberry Rosé

8 sugar cubes
1 cup cranberry juice
1 (750-milliliter) bottle sparkling extra-dry rosé
Fresh cranberries on skewers for garnish

Place 1 sugar cube in the bottom of each chilled Champagne flute. Pour 2 tablespoons cranberry juice into each glass. Fill each glass with some of the wine. Garnish each glass with a skewer of fresh cranberries. You may substitute Champagne or sparkling fruit juice for the rosé if desired.

Serves 8

HINT—For a special look, sprinkle colored sugar onto a piece of waxed paper. Moisten the rim of the Champagne flutes with water and dip each rim in the sugar. Let dry for 5 to 10 minutes before filling the glasses.

Perfect Lady

2 ounces gin
1 ounce Triple Sec
1/2 ounce sour mix

Combine the gin, Triple Sec and sour mix with ice in a shaker. Shake well and strain into a glass. Garnish with a strawberry.

Serves 1

Wassail

2 cinnamon sticks
1 teaspoon whole cloves
2 quarts apple juice
1 pint cranberry juice
3/4 cup packed brown sugar
1/2 to 1 cup rum (optional)

Combine the cinnamon sticks and whole cloves in a percolator basket. Place the apple juice, cranberry juice, brown sugar and rum in a percolator. Perk using the manufacturer's instructions. Serve hot.

Serves 12

Harvest Grains

Breads and Brunch

South Dakota Wheatfield • *Johnny Sundby, Dakota Skies Photography*

Prairies and grasslands are among South Dakota's greatest natural resources. Reflecting upon her life in South Dakota, American author Laura Ingalls Wilder wrote, "The prairie, the whole vast prairie, and the great sky and wind were clear and free." The natural prairies of our state are primarily composed of mixed grasses and tall grasses. These include western wheat grass, green needle grass, big and little bluestem, side-oats grama, porcupine grass, blue grama, and buffalo grass. There are nearly 21 million acres of mixed grass prairie and 1.2 million acres of tall grass prairie in South Dakota.

When black blizzards buried the Great Plains for nearly a decade during the Dust Bowl era, the National Grasslands Program was created. In response to the massive soil erosion, the United States government began purchasing land from homesteaders to conserve the wind-eroded lands. South Dakota's grasslands are used for watershed management, recreation, wildlife habitat, and hay production. However, livestock grazing is the most common use of our grasslands. The National Grassland Visitor Center is located in Wall, South Dakota.

South Dakota's prairies and grasslands have been celebrated in song and prose throughout history. Envision yourself walking through the amber waves of grain that blanket the prairies of our state as the aromas from these scrumptious bread and brunch recipes fill your kitchen.

Bananas Foster Waffles with Toasted Pecans

1 cup flour
1/2 cup pecans, toasted and finely chopped
1 teaspoon baking powder
1/4 teaspoon baking soda
1/2 teaspoon salt
1 cup buttermilk
1/2 cup (1 stick) butter, melted and divided
1 egg, lightly beaten
4 large bananas
3 tablespoons light brown sugar
1/4 teaspoon cinnamon
1/8 teaspoon nutmeg
1/4 cup dark rum
Vanilla ice cream or whipped cream

Preheat a waffle iron. Whisk the flour, pecans, baking powder, baking soda and salt together in a bowl. Add the buttermilk, 6 tablespoons of the melted butter and the egg and mix well. The batter will be thick. Pour 1/2 cup of the batter onto the hot waffle iron. Bake until brown using the manufacturer's directions. Place the waffles on a baking sheet and keep warm in a 250-degree oven. Repeat the process with the remaining batter.

Cut the bananas into quarters, halving lengthwise and crosswise. Heat the remaining 2 tablespoons butter in a large skillet over medium-low heat. Brown the bananas cut side down for 5 minutes. Turn and brown the other side for 5 minutes or just until fork-tender. Sprinkle with the brown sugar, cinnamon and nutmeg. Remove the bananas to a heatproof serving dish. Add the rum to the skillet and heat over medium heat, scraping the browned bits from the bottom of the skillet. Remove from the flame and ignite the rum using a long wooden match. Pour the rum over the bananas. Top the waffles with ice cream, rum sauce and bananas.

Makes 8 waffles

HINT—If you like your waffles on the crispy side, use less batter than the waffle iron directions suggest. Cook them for a few seconds longer after the steam has stopped.

Zandbroz Scone

3 cups flour
$1/3$ cup plus $1/4$ cup sugar, divided
$21/2$ teaspoons baking powder
$1/2$ teaspoon baking soda
$3/4$ teaspoon salt
$3/4$ cup ($11/2$ sticks) cold butter, cut into small pieces
1 tablespoon grated orange zest
1 cup (about) buttermilk
$1/4$ cup jam or jelly
$1/4$ cup ($1/2$ stick) butter, melted

Combine the flour, $1/3$ cup of the sugar, the baking powder, baking soda and salt in a food processor fitted with a steel blade. Pulse 4 or 5 times to combine. Add the cold butter pieces and pulse until the mixture resembles cornmeal. Stir the orange zest into the buttermilk and pour into the food processor. Pulse to form a rough dough. Do not let the dough form a ball.

Remove the dough to a lightly floured surface and press together. Knead the dough 10 to 12 times. Divide the dough in half and shape into 2 rounds. Roll 1 half into a $1/2$-inch-thick round on a lightly floured cutting board. Roll out the remaining dough to a slightly smaller round on a lightly floured surface. Spread the jam on the larger round, leaving a clean border. Top with the second round. Moisten the edges of the bottom round and pinch the edges over the top round to seal.

Line a baking sheet with parchment paper. Invert the baking sheet over the scone. Lift the cutting board and carefully turn it upside down onto the baking sheet. Remove the cutting board so that the scone is on the baking sheet, large round up. Brush the top of the scone with the melted butter and sprinkle with the remaining $1/4$ cup sugar. Cut through to the jam layer at intervals for decoration. Bake at 425 degrees for 16 to 18 minutes or until the top is light brown. Cut into wedges.

Serves 10 to 12

HINT—As an alternative to using a food processor, you may coarsely grate frozen butter into the flour mixture, tossing to mix several times during the process.

Nutty French Toast

8 eggs

2 cups milk

2 teaspoons vanilla extract

$1/2$ teaspoon cinnamon

12 (1-inch-thick) slices French bread

$3/4$ cup ($1^1/2$ sticks) butter or margarine, softened

$1^1/3$ cups packed brown sugar

3 tablespoons dark corn syrup

1 cup chopped walnuts

Beat the eggs, milk, vanilla and cinnamon together in a large mixing bowl. Arrange the bread in a greased 9×13-inch baking dish. Pour the egg mixture over the bread. Chill, covered, for 8 hours. Let the dish stand at room temperature for 30 minutes before baking. Cream the butter, brown sugar and corn syrup in a mixing bowl until smooth. Spread the butter mixture over the bread. Sprinkle with the walnuts. Bake at 350 degrees for 1 hour.

Serves 6 to 8

Sour Cream Berry Muffins

1/2 cup (1 stick) butter, softened
11/2 cups sugar
1/2 teaspoon salt
4 eggs, well beaten
11/2 cups sour cream
1 teaspoon baking soda
23/4 cups flour
1/2 teaspoon grated nutmeg
2 cups fresh or thawed frozen blueberries, raspberries,
    blackberries or a combination
Sugar for sprinkling

Cream the butter, 11/2 cups sugar and the salt at high speed in a mixing bowl until light and creamy. Beat in the eggs and sour cream. Sift the baking soda, flour and nutmeg together into a bowl. Add to the butter mixture and stir just until moistened. Add the berries and stir gently to combine.

Fill muffin cups sprayed with nonstick cooking spray 1/2 to 2/3 full. Sprinkle the muffins with additional sugar. Bake at 450 degrees for 12 to 15 minutes or until a wooden pick inserted in the center of a muffin comes out clean. Cool in the pan for 10 minutes. Remove to a wire rack to cool completely.

Makes 2 dozen

HINT—To make uniform-sized muffins, use an ice cream scoop to measure batter into muffin cups.

Carrot Rolls

2 cups milk
1 teaspoon salt
2 teaspoons dry yeast
2 tablespoons honey
2/3 cup finely grated carrots
2 cups rolled oats
3 to 3½ cups flour
¼ cup (½ stick) butter, melted

Pour the milk into a saucepan and heat to 110 degrees. Pour the warm milk into a mixing bowl. Add the salt, yeast, honey, carrots and oats and mix well. Add about half the flour. Knead the mixture. Add more flour gradually. When most of the flour has been added, mix in the melted butter. Knead for 5 minutes or until the dough is of a soft consistency, adding more flour if necessary. Place the dough in a greased bowl, turning to coat the surface. Let rise, covered, in a warm place for 45 to 60 minutes or until doubled in bulk.

Shape the dough into 20 to 24 flat rolls. Place on a parchment paper-lined baking sheet. Let rise for 45 minutes. Bake at 410 degrees for 12 to 15 minutes or until the rolls are golden brown. Remove the rolls from the baking sheet. Cool on a wire rack.

Makes 20 to 24 rolls

HINT—For a wonderful spread for the Carrot Rolls, mix 8 ounces softened cream cheese, 3/4 cup softened butter, 1 or 2 garlic cloves, 2 teaspoons mixed Italian herbs or 2 tablespoons minced fresh parsley and a pinch of salt. Chill for 1 hour before serving.

Grandma's Bread

1 envelope dry yeast
1/4 cup warm water
1 cup water
1 cup milk
2 tablespoons sugar
1/2 cup (1 stick) butter
1/3 cup instant mashed potato flakes
2 teaspoons salt
4 cups flour, divided
1 egg

Dissolve the yeast in the warm water in a small bowl and set aside. Heat 1 cup water and the milk in a saucepan until the milk is scalded. Add the sugar, butter, mashed potato flakes and salt to the scalded milk and mix well. Set aside to cool to room temperature.

Combine 2 cups of the flour and the milk mixture in a mixing bowl and beat until blended. Add the egg and mix well. Add the yeast mixture. Gradually add about 2 more cups flour, continuing to mix until the dough is no longer sticky. Place the dough in a floured bowl. Let rise, covered, in a warm place for 45 minutes or until doubled in bulk.

Punch the dough down. Let rise again, covered, for 45 minutes or until doubled in bulk. Punch the dough down again. Shape into rolls. Place the rolls on a greased baking sheet. Cover and let rise again until doubled in bulk. Bake at 350 degrees for 22 minutes. You may make bread loaves by shaping into loaves and placing in greased loaf pans. Let rise, covered, for 45 minutes or until doubled in bulk. Bake at 350 degrees for 32 minutes.

Makes 36 rolls or 3 loaves

HINT—To make caramel rolls, increase the sugar to 1/2 cup. Proceed with preparing the rolls. Combine 2 cups packed brown sugar, 1/2 cup white corn syrup and 1/4 cup evaporated milk in a bowl and mix well. Spread the mixture over the bottom of two 9×13-inch baking pans. Arrange the unbaked rolls in the prepared pans. Bake at 350 degrees for 22 minutes.

Oregano and Cheese Bread

2 cups milk or water
1¹/₂ teaspoons salt
2 teaspoons dry yeast
2 teaspoons oregano
4 cups bread flour

1 cup (4 ounces) shredded Swiss, or
    asiago or Italian cheese blend
¹/₄ cup (¹/₂ stick) butter, melted
Oregano

Pour the milk into a saucepan and heat to 110 degrees. Combine the warm milk with the salt, yeast and 2 teaspoons oregano in a mixing bowl and mix well. Add about half the flour. Using a dough hook, knead the mixture. Add most of the cheese. Add more flour gradually. When most of the flour has been added, mix in the melted butter. Knead for 5 minutes or until the dough is of a soft consistency, adding more flour if necessary. Place the dough in a greased bowl, turning to coat the surface. Let rise, covered, in a warm place for 45 to 60 minutes or until doubled in bulk.

Divide the dough into 30 pieces and roll into balls. Place 2 rows of 5 balls in each of 2 greased and floured 4×8-inch loaf pans. Add a second row of 5 balls in the center of each pan. Let rise, covered, for 45 minutes. Sprinkle the loaves with the remaining cheese and additional oregano. Bake at 410 degrees for 25 minutes or until golden brown. Cool in the pans for 10 minutes. Remove to a wire rack to cool completely.

Makes 2 loaves

Party Bread

1 (1-pound) round sourdough bread
16 ounces Monterey Jack cheese,
    sliced

¹/₂ cup (1 stick) butter, melted
¹/₂ cup chopped green onions
2 to 3 teaspoons poppy seeds

Make lengthwise and crosswise cuts in the bread, but do not slice through the bread. Place some of the cheese in each cut. Place the bread on a large sheet of foil on a baking sheet. Pour the butter over the bread. Sprinkle with the green onions and poppy seeds. Wrap the bread in the foil. Bake at 350 degrees for 15 minutes. Unwrap the bread and bake for 10 minutes longer.

Serves 6

Lemon Buttermilk Loaves

LOAVES

3½ cups flour
½ teaspoon baking soda
½ teaspoon salt
½ cup (1 stick) butter, softened
1 cup shortening
2½ cups sugar

4 eggs
1 teaspoon lemon extract
1 teaspoon vanilla extract
1 teaspoon water
1 cup buttermilk

LEMON GLAZE

Grated zest of 2 lemons
Juice of 2 lemons

½ cup sugar
½ teaspoon water

For the loaves, combine the flour, baking soda and salt in a bowl. Cream the butter, shortening and sugar in a mixing bowl until light and fluffy. Add the eggs 1 at a time, mixing well after each addition. Add the lemon extract, vanilla and water and mix well. Add the flour mixture alternately with the buttermilk while beating. Pour into 2 greased and floured loaf pans. Bake at 325 degrees for 1 hour to 1 hour and 15 minutes or until a wooden pick inserted in the center of the loaves comes out clean. Remove the pans from the oven and cool slightly on a wire rack.

For the glaze, combine the lemon zest, lemon juice, sugar and water in a bowl and stir until the sugar dissolves. Pour the glaze over the loaves. Remove the loaves to a wire rack to cool completely.

Makes 2 loaves

HINT—If you do not have buttermilk on hand, place 1 tablespoon vinegar or lemon juice in a measuring cup. Fill with milk to equal 1 cup. Stir and let the mixture stand for 5 minutes.

Orange-Glazed Poppy Seed Bread

BREAD

3 cups flour

1 1/2 teaspoons salt

1 1/2 teaspoons baking powder

3 eggs

2 1/4 cups sugar

1 1/2 teaspoons vanilla extract

1 1/2 teaspoons almond extract

1 1/2 teaspoons butter flavoring

1 tablespoon poppy seeds

3/4 cup vegetable oil

1 1/2 cups milk

ORANGE GLAZE

3/4 cup confectioners' sugar

1/2 teaspoon vanilla extract

1/2 teaspoon almond extract

1/2 teaspoon butter flavoring

1/2 cup orange juice

For the bread, combine the flour, salt, baking powder, eggs, sugar, vanilla, almond extract, butter flavoring, poppy seeds, oil and milk in a mixing bowl and beat for 1 to 2 minutes or until the batter is well mixed. Pour the batter into 2 greased loaf pans or 6 greased miniature loaf pans, filling no more than 2/3 full. Bake at 350 degrees for 1 hour for full-size loaves or for 30 to 35 minutes for miniature loaves or until a wooden pick inserted into the center of the loaves comes out clean. Remove from the oven and cool for 5 minutes.

For the glaze, whisk the confectioners' sugar, vanilla, almond extract, butter flavoring and orange juice together in a small bowl. Pour the glaze over the loaves. Cool completely in the pans. Loosen the edges with a knife and remove the loaves from the pans to slice.

Makes 2 large loaves or 6 miniature loaves

Pumpkin Roll

CAKE

3 eggs
1 cup sugar
2/3 cup pumpkin
1 teaspoon lemon juice
3/4 cup flour
1 teaspoon baking powder

2 teaspoons cinnamon
1 teaspoon ginger
1 teaspoon nutmeg
1/2 teaspoon salt
1 cup finely chopped walnuts
Confectioners' sugar

FILLING

1 cup confectioners' sugar
6 ounces cream cheese, softened

1/4 cup (1/2 stick) butter, softened
1/4 teaspoon vanilla extract

ASSEMBLY

Confectioners' sugar
Chopped walnuts

For the cake, beat the eggs at high speed in a mixing bowl for 5 minutes. Add the sugar, pumpkin and lemon juice and mix well. Combine the flour, baking powder, cinnamon, ginger, nutmeg and salt in a bowl. Fold into the pumpkin mixture. Spread the batter in a greased and floured 10×15-inch baking pan. Sprinkle with the walnuts. Bake at 375 degrees for 15 minutes. Dust a clean kitchen towel generously with confectioners' sugar. Invert the cake onto the towel. Roll the warm cake in the towel from the short side as for a jelly roll and place on a wire rack. Cool for 5 to 6 hours. Unroll the cooled cake carefully and remove the towel.

For the filling, combine the confectioners' sugar, cream cheese, butter and vanilla in a mixing bowl and beat until smooth. Spread the filling to within 1/2 inch of the edge of the cake and re-roll. Place seam side down on a serving plate.

To assemble, dust the roll with confectioners' sugar or spread with any leftover filling and sprinkle with chopped walnuts.

Serves 16

Blueberry Lattice Coffee Cake

CAKE

1 envelope dry yeast

1 teaspoon plus 1/4 cup sugar, divided

1/4 cup water (110 degrees)

1 egg, beaten

1/2 cup (1 stick) butter, softened

1/3 cup milk

3 to 31/2 cups flour

1/2 teaspoon salt

FILLING

16 ounces cream cheese, softened

2 egg yolks

2/3 cup sugar

1 teaspoon vanilla or lemon extract

1 teaspoon grated lemon zest

1 cup fresh or thawed frozen
blueberries

For the cake, dissolve the yeast and 1 teaspoon of the sugar in the warm water in a large mixing bowl. Let stand for 10 minutes. Beat in the egg, butter and milk. Beat in 3 cups flour, the remaining 1/4 cup sugar and salt to make a soft dough. Knead on a floured surface for 10 minutes or until smooth and elastic, adding more flour if necessary to prevent sticking. Place in a greased bowl. Cover and let the dough rest while making the filling.

For the filling, combine the cream cheese, egg yolks, sugar, vanilla and lemon zest in a mixing bowl and beat until light. Roll 2/3 of the dough into a 9×13-inch rectangle. Place in a greased 9×13-inch baking pan and press the dough 1/2 inch up the side. Spoon the filling into the dough-lined pan. Spread the blueberries over the filling, pressing lightly into the filling. Roll out the remaining 1/3 of the dough into a 10×10-inch square. Cut the dough into 1-inch strips. Arrange the strips diagonally in a lattice pattern over the filling. Seal the strips to the edge. Chill, covered with plastic wrap, for 2 to 8 hours.

Bake at 350 degrees for 40 minutes or until the top is light brown and the filling is set. Serve warm or at room temperature.

Serves 15

HINT—For a decorative touch, use a scalloped pastry wheel to cut out lattice dough strips.

Coffee Cake Crunch

1¹/₄ cups chopped pecans or walnuts, divided
1¹/₂ cups sugar, divided
1¹/₂ teaspoons cinnamon
¹/₂ cup (1 stick) butter or margarine, softened
1 teaspoon vanilla extract
2 eggs
1 cup sour cream
1¹/₂ cups flour
1¹/₂ teaspoons baking powder
1 teaspoon baking soda
Dash of salt

Combine ³/₄ cup of the pecans, ¹/₂ cup of the sugar and the cinnamon in a small bowl. Cream the butter, the remaining 1 cup sugar and the vanilla in a mixing bowl. Add the eggs and sour cream and stir just until mixed.

Combine the flour, baking powder, baking soda and salt in a small bowl. Gradually add to the creamed mixture, mixing until smooth. Stir in the remaining ¹/₂ cup chopped pecans. Pour half the batter into a greased 10-inch tube pan. Sprinkle with the pecan mixture. Pour the remaining batter over the pecan mixture. Bake at 350 degrees for 45 to 50 minutes or until a wooden pick inserted into the center comes out clean. Cool the cake in the pan. Invert onto a plate and glaze with a confectioners' sugar frosting.

Serves 10 to 12

HINT—For confectioners' sugar frosting, add milk to 2 cups confectioners' sugar for spreading consistency. Add a dash of salt and 1 teaspoon vanilla.

Almond Pear Buckle

2¹/4 cups flour, divided
1¹/4 cups packed brown sugar, divided
¹/2 teaspoon cinnamon, divided
1¹/4 teaspoons salt, divided
¹/4 cup (¹/2 stick) cold butter, cut into cubes
¹/2 cup sliced almonds, toasted
2 pears, peeled and chopped
1 tablespoon fresh lemon juice
2 teaspoons baking powder
¹/4 cup (¹/2 stick) butter, softened
1 egg, chilled
¹/2 teaspoon vanilla extract
¹/4 teaspoon almond extract
¹/2 cup half-and-half
Whipped cream for garnish

Combine ¹/2 cup of the flour, ¹/2 cup of the brown sugar, ¹/4 teaspoon of the cinnamon and ¹/4 teaspoon of the salt in a food processor and pulse 4 or 5 times to combine. Add the cold butter and pulse until the mixture resembles coarse bread crumbs. Combine the flour mixture and almonds in a bowl. Toss the pears and lemon juice in a bowl.

Combine the remaining 1³/4 cups flour, the baking powder, remaining ¹/4 teaspoon cinnamon and remaining 1 teaspoon salt in a mixing bowl. Combine the softened butter, remaining ³/4 cup brown sugar, egg, vanilla and almond extract in a mixing bowl and beat until light and fluffy. Gradually add the half-and-half, beating constantly. Add the flour mixture to the half-and-half mixture, stirring just until combined. Fold in the pears. Pour the batter into a buttered and floured 10-inch round baking pan or 9×9-inch baking pan and spread evenly. Top with the almond mixture. Bake at 350 degrees for 40 to 45 minutes or until the top springs back to the touch and a wooden pick inserted in the center comes out clean. Serve with whipped cream.

Serves 8

HINT—To enhance whipped cream, add your favorite liqueur or vanilla extract.

Norwegian Potato Lefse

5 pounds (about) russet potatoes, peeled and chopped
1 cup heavy cream
1/2 cup (1 stick) plus 2 tablespoons butter
1 1/4 teaspoons salt
1/3 cup sugar
2 1/2 cups (about) flour

Combine the potatoes with water to cover in a large saucepan. Bring to a boil and cook until fork-tender; drain. Pass the potatoes through a ricer or food mill while hot. Measure 8 cups of packed riced potatoes into a large bowl. Combine the cream, butter, salt and sugar in a small saucepan and heat until the butter melts and sugar dissolves, stirring frequently. Add to the potatoes and mix well. Spread the potato mixture in a 10×15-inch baking pan. Cover loosely with a clean kitchen towel and let cool to room temperature.

Divide the potato mixture into 2-cup portions. Add 1/2 cup flour to 1 portion at a time and knead until smooth. Do not add all the flour to the potato mixture at once or the dough will be sticky.

Form each dough portion into a log 2 1/2 inches in diameter. Slice into 1-inch pieces. Roll each piece into a ball and flatten into a small patty. Dust both sides with flour. Using a cloth-covered floured rolling pin, roll into a 12-inch circle on a well-floured pastry cloth. Transfer to a hot griddle using a lefse stick. Cook over high heat until the lefse is light brown and bubbly on both sides. Remove and cover loosely with a clean kitchen towel until cool. To prevent sticking, do not stack the lefse. Store cold lefse in sealable plastic bags with the air gently pressed out of the bags. Serve with butter and sugar.

Serves 36

HINT—Although lefse is time-consuming to make, it does freeze well, so it can be made in advance. A traditional Scandinavian treat, it is eaten during the holiday season.

Cheese and Spinach Pie

2 tablespoons butter or margarine
1/2 cup chopped onion
1/2 cup chopped green bell pepper
1 (10-ounce) package frozen chopped spinach, thawed and squeezed dry
2 tomatoes, peeled, seeded and chopped
2 teaspoons oregano, crushed
2 eggs
1 (10-ounce) can Cheddar cheese soup
1 cup plain yogurt
1/2 cup (2 ounces) crumbled feta cheese
1/4 cup flour
8 sheets frozen phyllo pastry, thawed
1/2 cup (1 stick) butter or margarine, melted

Melt 2 tablespoons butter in a medium skillet. Add the onion and bell pepper. Cook over medium-high heat until tender, stirring occasionally. Add the spinach, tomatoes and oregano. Remove from the heat. Beat the eggs in a mixing bowl. Add the soup, yogurt, cheese and flour and mix well. Fold in the spinach mixture.

Brush 1 sheet of the pastry with melted butter and fold in half to form a 3×8-inch rectangle. Place in a greased 7×12-inch baking dish. Repeat the process with 2 more sheets of pastry. Spoon the spinach mixture over the pastry. Brush the remaining sheets of pastry with the remaining butter. Fold each pastry sheet in half and place over the spinach filling, tucking in the edges. Bake at 325 degrees for 45 to 50 minutes or until the filling is set and the top is golden brown. Remove from the oven and let stand for 10 minutes before cutting into squares.

Serves 6

Quiche Lorraine

8 to 10 slices bacon, chopped
1 small onion, chopped
6 eggs
1 cup heavy cream
Dash of white pepper
Dash of cayenne pepper

1/4 teaspoon salt
1/8 teaspoon nutmeg
1 unbaked (9-inch) pie shell
2 cups (8 ounces) shredded Swiss
    cheese

Sauté the bacon and onion in a skillet until the bacon is crisp-cooked; drain. Combine the eggs, cream, white pepper, cayenne pepper, salt and nutmeg in a bowl and mix well. Bake the pie shell at 350 degrees for 4 minutes. Prick any bubbles in the pie shell and bake for 3 minutes longer. Spread the bacon mixture in the pie shell. Sprinkle with the cheese. Pour the egg mixture over the cheese. Bake at 350 degrees for 45 minutes or until a knife inserted near the center comes out clean.

Serves 6

Sausage Soufflé

1 pound bulk pork sausage
1 pound spicy bulk pork sausage
12 eggs
4 slices bread, cubed
4 cups milk

1 teaspoon salt
1 teaspoon dry mustard
2 cups (8 ounces) shredded Cheddar
    cheese

Brown the sausage in a skillet, stirring until crumbly; drain. Beat the eggs in a large mixing bowl until slightly frothy. Add the bread, milk, salt, dry mustard and sausage. Stir in the cheese. Pour into a 9×13-inch baking dish. Chill, covered, for 8 hours. Bake at 400 degrees for 45 minutes or until a knife inserted near the center comes out clean.

Serves 10 to 12

Frozen Fruit Cups

1 (17-ounce) can apricot halves
1 (20-ounce) can crushed pineapple
1/2 cup sugar
3 (10-ounce) cartons frozen sliced unsweetened strawberries, thawed
1 (6-ounce) can frozen orange juice concentrate, thawed
2 tablespoons lemon juice
3 bananas, sliced

Drain the apricots and pineapple, reserving the juice. Add enough of the pineapple juice to the apricot juice to measure 1 cup. Warm the apricot juice and sugar in a small saucepan over low heat until the sugar dissolves, stirring constantly. Cut the apricot halves into quarters. Combine the apricots, apricot juice mixture, strawberries, orange juice concentrate, lemon juice and bananas in a large bowl and mix well.

Spoon the fruit mixture into foil-lined muffin cups, filling 3/4 full. Freeze the muffin cups until solid. Remove the fruit from the muffin cups when solid and store in a sealable plastic bag in the freezer for up to 1 year. To serve, remove the foil liners and thaw the fruit until of a slushy consistency.

Serves 24

Strawberry and Banana Fruit Compote

FRUIT SAUCE

1 cup sour cream

$1/2$ cup strawberries

1 banana

2 tablespoons candied ginger

1 tablespoon brown sugar

1 tablespoon rum

COMPOTE AND ASSEMBLY

3 cups sliced bananas

2 cups sliced strawberries

2 cups grapes, whole or halved

Mint leaves

For the sauce, purée the sour cream, strawberries, banana, ginger, brown sugar and rum in a food processor. Chill, covered, for 8 to 12 hours.

For the compote, combine the bananas, strawberries and grapes in a large bowl. Stir in the sauce. Serve in 1 large bowl or individual dishes. Top with mint leaves.

Serves 4 to 6

City Lights

Soups and Salads

Sioux Falls Skyline • *Greg Latza, Peoplescapes Publishing*

Pictured here are the lights of Sioux Falls, the state's largest city, and home to more than 130,000 people. Today, our city is a far cry from the original frontier outpost that drew immigrants from Germany, Russia, Ireland, and Scandinavia during the last half of the nineteenth century. These settlers came to farm the land and harness the energy of the waterfalls of the Big Sioux River. Sioux Falls now offers its residents a multitude of cultural, recreational, and educational opportunities. Our economy is one of the most vibrant in the Midwest.

Throughout the year, we enjoy a variety of entertainment, from attending theater productions and art exhibits, to watching rodeos and other athletic events. Outdoor enthusiasts enjoy scenic trips along the bicycle trails that follow the Big Sioux River as it winds through the city. Residents also enjoy attending concerts in the parks, watching hot air balloons, or golfing on one of our many courses. It's no wonder Sioux Falls has consistently been rated as one of the best places to live in our country.

Other cities that shine brightly include Pierre, our state capital, centrally located on the banks of the Missouri River, and Rapid City, our second largest community, nestled in the beautiful Black Hills.

Every selection in this chapter may be served as a light meal or as a complement to your main course. These recipes include salads, perfect for hot summer days, and hearty soups to warm up cold winter days. As you prepare these dishes, may the warmth of family and friends gathered around your table cast a glow as bright as the city lights of our great state.

Elegant Cream of Mushroom Soup

1/4 cup (1/2 stick) butter, or more
1 onion, chopped
8 ounces white mushrooms
2 or 3 portobello mushrooms, sliced
1/4 cup flour
2 tablespoons chopped fresh parsley
2 teaspoons sage

1 teaspoon rosemary, finely ground
1 teaspoon whole-leaf thyme
4 cups milk
2 cups heavy cream
Salt and pepper to taste
1 to 3 tablespoons cornstarch dissolved
    in cold water

Melt the butter in a saucepan over medium-high heat. Add the onion and sauté until translucent. Finely chop half the white mushrooms. Remove the stems from the remaining white mushrooms and slice the mushroom caps. Add the chopped mushrooms, mushroom caps and portobello mushrooms to the onion and sauté until tender, adding additional butter if the pan is dry. Add the flour and stir until of a paste consistency. Add the parsley, sage, rosemary and thyme and cook for 1 to 2 minutes. Add the milk and bring just to a boil, stirring constantly. Add the cream and simmer until hot, stirring frequently. Increase the heat and bring the soup almost to a boil. Sprinkle with salt and pepper. Add enough of the cornstarch mixture to give the soup a slightly thick texture, stirring constantly. This soup may be frozen.

Serves 8 to 10

Cream of Salmon Soup

8 ounces cream cheese, softened
1 cup milk
1 teaspoon Dijon mustard
1/2 teaspoon dill weed

2 green onions, sliced
1 (14-ounce) can chicken broth
12 ounces smoked salmon

Combine the cream cheese, milk, Dijon mustard, dill weed, green onions and chicken broth in a saucepan and heat over medium heat for 5 to 10 minutes or until the cheese is melted. Cut the salmon into bite-size pieces. Add to the soup and cook until heated through, stirring frequently. Ladle into soup bowls or hollowed-out bread bowls.

Serves 4

Tomato Bisque

2 tablespoons olive oil
1 small onion, chopped
1 garlic clove, minced
3 sprigs of fresh thyme
1 (28-ounce) can tomatoes
1 1/2 cups chicken broth
3 tablespoons honey

1 1/2 teaspoons coarse salt, or to taste
1/4 teaspoon finely ground pepper, or
    to taste
1/4 cup heavy cream (optional)
2 tablespoons chopped fresh parsley
    (optional)

Heat the olive oil in a large saucepan. Add the onion and cook over medium heat for 8 minutes or until light brown. Add the garlic and thyme and cook for 1 minute or until fragrant, stirring constantly. Add the tomatoes, chicken broth, honey, salt and pepper. Bring the soup to a boil. Reduce the heat to low and simmer for 15 minutes or until the soup is reduced by 1/4. Pour the soup into a blender or food processor and process briefly. Do not purée. Pour into soup bowls. Add 1 tablespoon cream and 1 1/2 teapoons parsley to each serving if desired. You may serve the soup hot or cold.

Serves 4

Tomato Florentine Soup

1 tablespoon olive oil
1/2 cup chopped onion
2 garlic cloves, minced
1/2 teaspoon basil
1/2 teaspoon oregano
2 (14-ounce) cans chicken broth
2 (14-ounce) cans diced tomatoes

4 cups chopped spinach
Salt and pepper to taste
1/3 cup uncooked shell pasta
2 teaspoons balsamic vinegar
Sour cream to taste (optional)
Grated Parmesan cheese to taste
    (optional)

Heat the olive oil in a saucepan. Add the onion and sauté over medium-high heat until softened. Add the garlic. Sauté for 5 minutes or until the onion is translucent and the garlic is fragrant. Add the basil, oregano, chicken broth, tomatoes, spinach, salt and pepper. Bring the soup to a boil over high heat. Reduce the heat to low and stir in the pasta. Simmer, covered, for 15 to 20 minutes. Add the vinegar just before serving. Ladle into soup bowls. Top with a spoonful of sour cream and/or Parmesan cheese.

Serves 4

Vegetable Beef Soup

16 cups water
1 (12-ounce) can tomato paste
2 tablespoons sugar
1 bay leaf
1¹/₂ tablespoons parsley
4 pounds boneless beef chuck, cut into 1-inch pieces
1 onion, chopped
6 potatoes, cubed
8 ounces sliced carrots
2 (14-ounce) cans choice-cut tomatoes
1 cup sliced celery
1 small head cabbage, cored and shredded
6 beef bouillon cubes
Salt and pepper to taste

Bring the water to a boil in a 12-quart stockpot. Add the tomato paste, sugar, bay leaf and parsley and mix well. Add the beef, onion, potatoes, carrots, tomatoes, celery, cabbage and bouillon cubes. Bring the soup to a boil. Reduce the heat and simmer for 2 to 2¹/₂ hours, stirring every 30 minutes. Remove the bay leaf. Season with salt and pepper.

Serves 6 to 8

HINT—To remove fat from a soup or stew when you don't have time to chill the soup first, skim a slice of bread across the surface of the soup to soak up as much fat as possible.

Creamy Wild Rice Soup

1/2 cup (1 stick) butter
1 large onion, chopped
1/2 green bell pepper, chopped
1 1/2 ribs celery, chopped
1 (4-ounce) can sliced mushrooms, drained
1 cup flour
8 cups chicken broth
2 cups cooked wild rice
Salt and pepper to taste
1 cup half-and-half
1 to 2 tablespoons dry white wine (optional)
1 cup sliced almonds

Melt the butter in a large saucepan over medium-high heat. Add the onion, bell pepper, celery and mushrooms and sauté for 3 minutes or until the vegetables are tender. Sprinkle the flour over the vegetables and mix well. Do not let the mixture brown. Add the chicken broth slowly, stirring until the mixture is blended. Add the wild rice, salt and pepper. Simmer until the soup is heated through. Stir in the half-and-half and wine. Heat over low heat, but do not let the soup boil. Ladle into bowls and sprinkle with the sliced almonds just before serving.

Serves 10 to 12

Cheddar and Ham Chowder

2 cups water
2 cups cubed potatoes
1/2 cup sliced carrots
1/2 cup sliced celery
1/4 cup chopped onion
1 teaspoon salt
1/4 teaspoon pepper
1/4 cup (1/2 stick) butter
1/4 cup flour
2 cups milk
2 cups (8 ounces) shredded Cheddar cheese
1 (16-ounce) can whole kernel corn, drained
1 1/2 cups chopped cooked ham

Combine the water, potatoes, carrots, celery, onion, salt and pepper in a large saucepan and bring to a boil over high heat. Reduce the heat to low. Cover and simmer for 8 to 10 minutes or just until the vegetables are tender. Remove from the heat. Do not drain.

Melt the butter in a medium saucepan over medium heat. Stir in the flour and mix until of a paste consistency. Add the milk and cook until thickened and bubbly, stirring constantly. Add the cheese and heat until the cheese is melted, stirring constantly. Pour the cheese mixture into the vegetables and mix well. Warm the mixture over low heat. Add the corn and ham and cook until heated through, stirring occasionally.

Serves 6 to 8

Mexican Chicken Corn Chowder

1¹/₂ pounds boneless skinless
   chicken breasts
3 tablespoons butter or margarine
¹/₂ cup chopped onion
1 or 2 garlic cloves, minced
2 chicken bouillon cubes
1 cup hot water
¹/₂ to 1 teaspoon ground cumin
2 cups half-and-half

2 cups (8 ounces) shredded Monterey
   Jack cheese
1 (17-ounce) can cream-style corn
1 (4-ounce) can diced green chiles
¹/₄ to 1 teaspoon hot red pepper sauce
1 tomato, chopped
Fresh chopped cilantro for garnish
Fresh chopped parsley for garnish

Cut the chicken into bite-size pieces. Melt the butter in a large saucepan over medium heat. Add the chicken, onion and garlic and cook until brown. Dissolve the bouillon cubes in the hot water and add to the saucepan. Add the cumin. Bring the chicken mixture to a boil. Reduce the heat to low and simmer for 5 minutes. Add the half-and-half, cheese, corn, green chiles and red pepper sauce. Simmer until the cheese is melted. Stir in the tomato. Garnish with chopped fresh cilantro or parsley.

Serves 6 to 8

Oyster Stew

1 pint shucked fresh oysters, or
   3 (8-ounce) cans oysters
2 tablespoons butter
¹/₈ teaspoon seasoned salt

¹/₈ teaspoon parsley
16 cups (1 gallon) milk or a
   combination of milk and fat-free
   half-and-half

Combine the oysters, butter, seasoned salt and parsley in a saucepan. Cook over low heat until the edges of the oysters curl up. Remove from the heat. Heat the milk in a large heavy saucepan over low heat. Add the oysters and cook until the milk is hot, stirring frequently; do not scorch.

Serves 10

White Chicken Chili

8 cups (2 quarts) water
2 to 3 pounds boneless skinless
　　chicken breasts, cut into
　　bite-size pieces
2 tablespoons olive oil
2¹/₂ cups chopped onions
4 garlic cloves, chopped
2 jalapeño chiles, chopped
¹/₄ cup flour

1¹/₂ teaspoons white pepper
1¹/₂ teaspoons cumin
1 teaspoon salt
1 (4-ounce) can diced green chiles
2 (15-ounce) cans white kidney beans
Shredded Monterey Jack cheese
Salsa
Shredded lettuce

Bring the water to a boil in a large saucepan over high heat. Add the chicken and cook for 40 to 45 minutes or until cooked through. Skim off the fat. Reserve 3 cups of the chicken broth; discard the remainder or reserve for another use. Set the chicken and 3 cups reserved broth aside to cool. Heat the olive oil in a large saucepan over high heat. Add the onions, garlic and jalapeño chiles and sauté for 1 minute. Add the flour, white pepper, cumin and salt and mix to a paste consistency. Stir in the reserved broth and green chiles. Cook over medium heat until thick, stirring constantly. Add the chicken and beans. Sprinkle the chili with Monterey Jack cheese and top with salsa and shredded lettuce.

Serves 10

HINT—A fast and painless way to chop onions is to use a blender. Quarter the onions, place in the blender, and cover with water. Chop at high speed to the desired consistency. Strain the onions through a colander to drain the liquid.

Sturgis Chili

1 1/2 tablespoons vegetable oil
1/2 cup chopped onion
2 garlic cloves, minced
1 1/2 pounds ground beef
1 teaspoon salt, or to taste
1/2 teaspoon pepper, or to taste
2 tablespoons chili powder
2 teaspoons Mexican oregano
1 (15-ounce) can pinto beans, drained
   and rinsed

1 (14-ounce) can diced tomatoes
1 1/4 cups beer
1 ounce whiskey
2 teaspoons sugar
1 tablespoon masa harina dissolved in
   1/4 cup warm water
Tortilla chips
1 red onion, chopped
1 cup (4 ounces) shredded sharp
   Cheddar cheese

Heat the oil in a large Dutch oven over medium-high heat. Sauté the onion and garlic in the oil until tender. Add the ground beef and cook until the ground beef begins to brown. Add the salt, pepper, chili powder and oregano and cook until the ground beef is crumbly, stirring constantly; drain. Add the beans, tomatoes, beer, whiskey and sugar. Simmer for 30 minutes, stirring frequently. Stir in the masa harina mixture and cook for 7 to 10 minutes. Adjust the seasonings. Serve the chili on a bed of tortilla chips. Sprinkle the chili with the red onion and cheese.

Serves 8

HINT—To re-crisp soggy tortilla chips or crackers, spread on a baking sheet and warm in a 300-degree oven for 5 minutes or until crisp.

Roquefort Waldorf Salad on Mixed Greens

ROQUEFORT VINAIGRETTE
1 cup (4 ounces) Roquefort cheese or blue cheese
1 teaspoon minced fresh garlic
1 teaspoon coarsely ground pepper
1/2 teaspoon tarragon
1/2 teaspoon basil
1/2 teaspoon salt
3 tablespoons red wine vinegar
1 cup olive oil

SALAD
1 cup chopped Granny Smith apple
1 cup chopped Red Delicious apple
3/4 cup toasted chopped pecans
1/2 cup minced celery
1/4 cup thinly sliced scallions
1 tablespoon minced fresh parsley
Salt and pepper to taste
4 cups mixed baby salad greens
8 Belgian endive leaves, sliced crosswise

For the vinaigrette, crumble the cheese into a glass jar with a tight-fitting lid. Add the garlic, pepper, tarragon, basil, salt, vinegar and olive oil and seal the jar. Shake vigorously before using.

For the salad, combine the apples, pecans, celery, scallions and parsley in a large bowl and mix well. Add 1/2 cup of the Roquefort Vinaigrette to the apple mixture, including cheese chunks from the dressing. Toss lightly and season with salt and pepper. Combine the salad greens and Belgian endive in a large decorative bowl. Add 1/2 cup of the Roquefort Vinaigrette and toss. Mound the apple mixture in the center of the mixed greens.

Serves 4

Bok Choy Salad

1 head bok choy or spinach leaves, shredded or chopped
1 cup (4 ounces) shredded mozzarella cheese
1/2 small onion, finely chopped
1/4 cup sunflower seeds
1 (8-ounce) can sliced water chestnuts, drained
1/2 cup mayonnaise
1/4 cup soy sauce
1/4 cup packed brown sugar

Toss the bok choy, cheese, onion, sunflower seeds and water chestnuts together in a salad bowl. Whisk the mayonnaise, soy sauce and brown sugar together in a small bowl. Drizzle the mayonnaise dressing over the salad just before serving.

Serves 6 to 8

Broccoli Raisin Salad

1 bunch broccoli, cut into florets (about 4 cups)
1 pound bacon, crisp-cooked and crumbled
1/2 cup raisins, simmered in water and drained
1 small red onion, chopped
2 cups chopped celery
1 cup sunflower seeds
2 cups red grapes, halved
1 1/2 cups mayonnaise
1/3 cup sugar
4 1/2 tablespoons vinegar

Combine the broccoli, bacon, raisins, red onion, celery, sunflower seeds and grapes in a large bowl. Whisk the mayonnaise, sugar and vinegar together in a small bowl. Gently stir the dressing into the salad. Chill, covered, for 3 to 8 hours, stirring occasionally.

Serves 6 to 8

Apple Snicker Salad

1 (3-ounce) package French vanilla instant pudding mix
1 cup milk
1 (8-ounce) container frozen whipped topping, thawed
2 Granny Smith apples, cut into bite-size pieces
3 (2-ounce) Snickers bars, cut into bite-size pieces

Beat the pudding mix and milk in a mixing bowl. Fold in the whipped topping. Stir in the apples and Snickers bars just before serving.

Serves 6

Fresh Cranberry Salad

2 (12-ounce) packages fresh cranberries
1 large orange
2 cups sugar
1 (6-ounce) package raspberry or cherry gelatin
1 cup boiling water
1 (20-ounce) can crushed pineapple, drained
Chopped pecans (optional)

Mince the cranberries and unpeeled orange in a food processor. Combine the mixture with the sugar in a large bowl and mix well. Dissolve the gelatin in the boiling water in a heatproof bowl. Add the gelatin to the cranberry mixture and mix well. Stir in the pineapple and walnuts. Chill, covered, for 8 hours.

Serves 10

Orange Almond Salad

TARRAGON DRESSING
1 teaspoon tarragon
1/2 teaspoon Dijon mustard
1/2 teaspoon salt
1/8 teaspoon pepper
1 tablespoon sugar
1/2 cup tarragon wine vinegar
1 cup vegetable oil

SALAD
1 head romaine, chilled
1 (8-ounce) can mandarin oranges, drained
1/2 cup sliced almonds
4 slices bacon, crisp-cooked and crumbled

For the dressing, combine the tarragon, Dijon mustard, salt, pepper and sugar in a bowl and whisk until blended. Whisk in the vinegar, then the oil.

For the salad, tear the lettuce into bite-size pieces. Arrange on a large salad plate. Add the mandarin oranges. Drizzle with the desired amount of dressing. Sprinkle with the almonds and bacon. Chill, covered, for 20 minutes before serving.

Serves 4

HINT—To reduce the fat in homemade salad dressings, replace some of the oil with reduced-fat or fat-free vegetable broth, vegetable juice, tomato juice, wine, fruit nectar, or water. Using ground or prepared mustard also adds to the flavor and keeps the dressing from separating.

Winter Pear Salad

RASPBERRY VINAIGRETTE
1/2 cup raspberry vinegar
1/2 cup olive oil
1 teaspoon salt
1 teaspoon freshly ground pepper

SALAD
8 cups torn romaine and radicchio
8 pears, cored and thinly sliced
1 cup (4 ounces) crumbled Gorgonzola cheese
2 cups toasted walnuts
1/2 cup chopped fresh Italian parsley
1 cup raspberries

For the vinaigrette, combine the vinegar, olive oil, salt and ground pepper in a jar with a tight-fitting lid. Seal the jar and shake to combine. Chill until ready to serve.

For the salad, arrange the romaine and radicchio on a large serving plate. Arrange the pear slices over the lettuce. Crumble the cheese over the pears. Sprinkle with the walnuts, parsley and raspberries. Drizzle with the vinaigrette just before serving.

Serves 15

Strawberry Almond Salad

POPPY SEED DRESSING

1/3 cup sugar

2 tablespoons poppy seeds

2 tablespoons cider vinegar

1/4 cup milk

3/4 cup mayonnaise

2 teaspoons almond extract

SALAD

1/2 cup sliced almonds

3 tablespoons sugar

10 ounces romaine salad greens, torn into bite-size pieces

3 green onions, sliced

1 pint strawberries, sliced

For the dressing, combine the sugar, poppy seeds, vinegar, milk, mayonnaise and almond extract in a bowl and mix well. Chill, covered, until ready to serve.

For the salad, heat the almonds and sugar in a heavy saucepan until the sugar melts and the almonds are glazed and light brown, stirring constantly. Remove the pan from the heat immediately and let cool.

Toss the romaine salad greens, green onions and strawberries together in a large salad bowl. Add the dressing just before serving. Sprinkle with the almonds.

Serves 4 to 6

Sweet Potato Salad

1 sweet potato
1 white potato
1/4 cup chopped red onion

1/3 cup chopped celery
1/2 cup coleslaw dressing
Salt and pepper to taste

Combine the sweet potato and white potato with enough water to cover in a saucepan. Bring to a boil. Boil until tender; drain. Cool for a few minutes. Peel the potatoes and cut into 1/2-inch pieces. Combine the potatoes, red onion and celery in a bowl. Add the coleslaw dressing and toss gently to combine. Season with salt and pepper. Chill, covered, for several hours before serving.

Serves 4 to 6

HINT—To prepare the potatoes ahead of time, peel and place in a bowl of cold water. Cover the potatoes and refrigerate. This keeps the potatoes from turning dark. When you are ready to boil the potatoes, add a teaspoon of vinegar to the cooking water to create a light crust that helps the potatoes hold their shape when cut up and used in salads.

Lemon Basil Pasta Salad

16 ounces rotini
Grated zest of 1 lemon
1/4 cup lemon juice
1/3 cup extra-virgin olive oil
3 tomatoes, chopped

2 teaspoons basil
1 cup (4 ounces) freshly grated
    Parmesan cheese
2 teaspoons salt
2 teaspoons pepper

Cook the pasta using the package directions until al dente; drain. Toss the pasta with the lemon zest, lemon juice and olive oil in a large bowl. Chill, covered, in the refrigerator. Add the tomatoes, basil, cheese, salt and pepper and toss to combine. Chill, covered, until ready to serve.

Serves 4

Mediterranean Pasta Salad

GARLIC VINAIGRETTE

2 cups olive oil

2/3 cup red wine vinegar

5 garlic cloves, minced

1 1/2 teaspoons oregano

1 1/2 teaspoons salt

SALAD

32 ounces rotelle (small wheel pasta)

2 teaspoons vinegar

4 cups (16 ounces) crumbled
  feta cheese

1 (6-ounce) can sliced black olives

4 pints cherry tomatoes, halved

4 green bell peppers, cut into
  1/4-inch strips

4 red bell peppers, cut into
  1/4-inch strips

3 small cucumbers, sliced

2 (14-ounce) cans artichoke hearts,
  drained and quartered

2 pounds salami, sliced

1 red onion, thinly sliced

20 kalamata olives, pitted

2 or 3 small zucchini, sliced

For the vinaigrette, combine the olive oil, vinegar, garlic, oregano and salt in a bowl and mix well. Chill, covered, until ready to use.

For the salad, cook the pasta using the package directions until al dente; drain. Combine the pasta with the vinegar in a large bowl and toss to coat. Add the cheese, black olives, tomatoes, bell peppers, cucumbers, artichoke hearts, salami, red onion, kalamata olives and zucchini and mix well. Stir in the vinaigrette. Chill, covered, until ready to serve.

Serves 20

Spicy Peanut Noodles

1/4 cup corn oil

3 tablespoons sesame oil

1 teaspoon crushed red pepper flakes

3 tablespoons honey

2 tablespoons soy sauce

1 teaspoon salt

8 ounces spaghetti, cooked and drained

2 tablespoons chopped fresh cilantro

1/4 cup roasted chopped peanuts

1/4 cup minced green onions

1 tablespoon toasted sesame seeds

Cilantro leaves for garnish

Combine the corn oil, sesame oil and red pepper flakes in a saucepan over medium heat. Cook for 2 minutes, stirring frequently. Stir in the honey, soy sauce and salt. Combine the pasta with the soy sauce mixture in a large bowl and mix well. Chill, covered, for 4 to 8 hours. Add the cilantro, peanuts and green onions to the pasta and toss. Sprinkle each serving with some of the sesame seeds and garnish with cilantro leaves.

Serves 4

Shrimp and Asparagus Penne Salad

DILL DRESSING

1/2 cup olive oil

1/2 cup rice wine vinegar

1 garlic clove, crushed

1 teaspoon red pepper flakes

1 tablespoon dried dill weed

1 tablespoon sugar

SALAD

1 pound asparagus

1 small bunch broccoli

16 ounces penne, cooked and drained

12 to 15 peeled cooked medium shrimp

1 red bell pepper, sliced

6 to 8 mushrooms, sliced

1/2 cup (2 ounces) grated Parmesan cheese

For the dressing, combine the olive oil, vinegar, garlic, red pepper flakes, dill weed and sugar in a bowl and whisk to combine. Chill, covered, until ready to serve.

For the salad, steam the asparagus and broccoli until tender-crisp; drain. Plunge immediately into cold water to stop the cooking process. Cut the asparagus and broccoli into bite-size pieces. Combine the pasta with the asparagus and broccoli in a large bowl and toss to combine. Add the shrimp, bell pepper and mushrooms. Pour the dressing over the pasta and toss gently to coat. Sprinkle with the cheese.

Serves 8 to 10

Wild Rice and Chicken Salad

3 cups water
1/2 teaspoon salt
1 tablespoon butter
1 cup long grain wild rice
1/4 cup orange juice
1 1/2 tablespoons white wine vinegar
1 tablespoon Dijon mustard
2 large garlic cloves, crushed
1/2 teaspoon ground pepper
1 1/2 tablespoons olive oil
1 pound cubed cooked chicken breast
1 red bell pepper, cut into 1/2-inch pieces
6 green onions, sliced
1/2 cup chopped fresh basil
2 tablespoons capers
3 cups chopped romaine

Bring the water, salt and butter to a boil in a medium saucepan. Stir in the wild rice. Reduce the heat to low and simmer, covered, for 1 hour. Whisk the orange juice, vinegar, Dijon mustard, garlic, pepper and olive oil together in a large bowl. Add the cooked rice, chicken, bell pepper, green onions, basil and capers and mix well. Add the romaine and toss to combine.

Serves 4 to 6

HINT—For homemade salad croutons, cut soft bread into bite-size squares. Brush the bread with butter or olive oil, season to taste, and arrange on a baking sheet. Bake at 350 degrees for 20 minutes or until light brown.

Oriental Chicken Salad

ORIENTAL DRESSING

1/2 cup sugar

1 tablespoon cornstarch

1/4 cup water

1/4 cup vegetable oil

1/4 cup ketchup

3 tablespoons cider vinegar

1 tablespoon soy sauce

SALAD

1 head lettuce, torn into bite-size pieces

2 cups chopped cooked chicken

1 cup salted cashews

1 (8-ounce) can sliced water chestnuts, drained

1 (6-ounce) package frozen snow peas, thawed

1 (3-ounce) can chow mein noodles

1/4 cup chopped green onions

For the dressing, combine the sugar, cornstarch, water, oil, ketchup, vinegar and soy sauce in a small saucepan. Bring to a boil. Cook for 2 minutes or until thickened, stirring constantly. Remove from the heat and let stand until cool.

For the salad, combine the lettuce, chicken, cashews, water chestnuts, snow peas, chow mein noodles and green onions in a large salad bowl and mix well. Add the dressing and toss to coat. Serve immediately.

Serves 8 to 10

Main Carvings

Meats and Entrées

Mount Rushmore National Memorial • *Johnny Sundby, Dakota Skies Photography*

South Dakota is known for its "Great Faces and Great Places." Among these are Mount Rushmore National Memorial and Crazy Horse Memorial. Both mountain carvings are located in the Black Hills of South Dakota and attract more than two million visitors to our state each year.

Mount Rushmore National Memorial was built during the years spanning from 1927 to 1941 by Gutzon Borglum, along with a team of more than 400 workers. This mountain carving depicts American Presidents George Washington, Thomas Jefferson, Theodore Roosevelt, and Abraham Lincoln. The monument honors the four presidents for providing hope, will, determination, and dreams for the people of our great nation.

Crazy Horse Memorial was begun in 1947 when Chief Henry Standing Bear collaborated with sculptor Korczak Ziolkowski to design a tribute to the legendary Lakota leader, Crazy Horse. Korczak created a scale model to honor the leader and, based on this model, he began his work on the mountain carving. In 1982, Korczak died, but his dream lives on today through his wife, Ruth, and their ten children. Although no specific completion date is projected, this carving will be taller than the Washington Monument when finished. Alone, the head of Crazy Horse will be larger than all four faces of Mount Rushmore.

As the centerpiece of your meal, the meats and entrées in this chapter are as impressive as our spectacular monuments. When you prepare these recipes for the great faces in your life, your table is sure to be a great place to dine.

Royal Beef Tenderloin

BEEF

1 cup soy sauce

2/3 cup vegetable oil

3 tablespoons brown sugar

2 tablespoons Dijon mustard

1 tablespoon white wine vinegar

1 teaspoon garlic powder

1 green onion, chopped

1 (5- to 6-pound) beef tenderloin, trimmed

ROYAL BUTTER

1/2 cup (1 stick) butter or margarine, softened

8 ounces cream cheese, softened

1/4 cup mayonnaise

1/4 cup horseradish, drained

Cremini mushrooms for garnish

Flat-leaf parsley for garnish

For the beef, combine the soy sauce, oil, brown sugar, Dijon mustard, vinegar, garlic powder and green onion in a sealable plastic bag and mix well. Add the tenderloin and seal. Marinate in the refrigerator for 8 hours, turning occasionally. Drain the tenderloin, reserving the marinade. Place the reserved marinade in a small saucepan. Bring to a boil. Boil for 2 to 3 minutes, stirring constantly.

Place the tenderloin on a rack in a roasting pan. Roast at 400 degrees for 1 hour or until a meat thermometer inserted into the thickest portion registers 145 degrees for rare, 160 degrees for medium or until done to taste, basting occasionally with the reserved marinade. Let stand for 10 minutes before carving.

For the Royal Butter, beat the butter, cream cheese, mayonnaise and horseradish in a mixing bowl. Serve the tenderloin with the Royal Butter and garnish with cremini mushrooms and flat-leaf parsley.

Serves 10

HINT—Sealable plastic bags in various sizes are great for marinating meat. Once sealed, you can shake the bag to make sure the marinade covers the meat. Sealable plastic bags take up little space in the refrigerator.

Grilled Peppered Steaks

3/4 cup olive oil

1/3 cup red wine vinegar

4 1/2 tablespoons Dijon mustard

4 large garlic cloves, minced

2 large shallots or green onions, chopped

4 teaspoons pepper

1 tablespoon minced fresh rosemary, or 1 teaspoon crumbled dried rosemary

1 teaspoon salt

1 tablespoon minced fresh thyme, or 1 teaspoon dried thyme

3 flank steaks (about 1 1/4 pounds each)

Pepper to taste

Rosemary sprigs for garnish

Thyme sprigs for garnish

Whisk the olive oil, vinegar, Dijon mustard, garlic, shallots, pepper, rosemary, salt and thyme together in a bowl. Pour into a large pan or sealable plastic bag. Add the steaks, turning to coat. Marinate, covered, in the refrigerator for 8 hours. Remove the steaks from the marinade, discarding the marinade, and season generously on both sides with additional pepper. Grill the steaks over medium-hot coals to medium doneness. Let stand for 10 minutes before carving. Cut the steaks crossgrain. Garnish with rosemary and thyme sprigs.

Serves 8

HINT—You can substitute buffalo in any of your beef recipes. There is no gamy taste, and you get more protein and less fat and cholesterol than with beef. Here are a few cooking tips: When broiling, add some water to the roasting pan, move your broiler rack a notch further away from the heat source, and reduce the temperature to 275 degrees to prevent the meat from drying out. When grilling, use a lower temperature and turn the buffalo sooner than you would beef.

Teriyaki Flank Steak

2 pounds flank steak, cut into
    1-inch strips
3/4 cup vegetable oil
1/2 cup soy sauce
2 tablespoons honey
2 tablespoons vinegar
1 1/2 teaspoons ground ginger
1 teaspoon garlic powder
1 green onion, chopped

Roll each beef strip and secure with a wooden pick. Place the rolls in a large glass dish. Combine the oil, soy sauce, honey, vinegar, ground ginger, garlic powder and green onion in a bowl and mix well. Pour over the beef. Marinate, covered, in the refrigerator for 8 hours. Drain the beef, discarding the marinade. Place on a grill over medium-hot coals or on a rack in a broiler pan. Grill or broil the steak for 10 minutes on each side or to the desired degree of doneness.

Serves 4

HINT—This marinade is also great with chicken. Use half the amount of the marinade for 4 boneless chicken breasts. Marinate overnight, then grill or broil for 10 minutes per side. Makes great chicken sandwiches.

Dakota Beef Stew

4 tablespoons (1/2 stick) butter or margarine, divided
2 pounds (1-inch) lean stew meat
2 tablespoons flour
1 cup burgundy
1 cup water
1 beef bouillon cube
1 cup sliced onion
2 garlic cloves, minced
2 carrots, sliced
Salt and pepper to taste
3 tablespoons brandy
2 sprigs of parsley
1 or 2 sprigs of thyme
1 bay leaf
Water or wine
Hot cooked mashed potatoes

Melt 3 tablespoons of the butter in a large skillet. Add the beef and brown on all sides. Remove the beef to a greased 1 1/2-quart baking dish. Stir the flour into the drippings in the skillet and brown over low heat, stirring frequently. Add the wine, water and bouillon cube. Cook over low heat until the bouillon cube is dissolved, stirring frequently. Pour the wine mixture over the beef. Melt the remaining 1 tablespoon butter in the skillet. Add the onion, garlic and carrots and sauté until brown. Add the vegetables to the beef. Add the salt, pepper and brandy. Place the parsley, thyme and bay leaf in a tea ball and add to the beef. Add enough additional water or wine to cover the beef. Bake, covered, at 300 degrees for 3 hours. Remove the tea ball and discard the herbs. Serve over mashed potatoes.

Serves 6

Spicy Shredded Beef

2 tablespoons vegetable oil
1 pound beef chuck, trimmed and
    cut into 1-inch cubes
1 garlic clove, minced
1/2 teaspoon salt

1/2 teaspoon cumin
1 serrano chile, minced, or 1/4 teaspoon
    chile paste
1 (15-ounce) can diced tomatoes

Heat the oil in a large skillet over medium-high heat. Add the beef and cook for 10 to 12 minutes or until brown; reduce the heat. Add the garlic, salt, cumin and serrano chile and simmer for 15 minutes, stirring occasionally. Add the undrained tomatoes and bring to a boil. Reduce the heat to low. Cook, covered, for 1 1/2 hours or until the beef is very tender. Add water as needed so the beef doesn't become dry. Cool the beef and shred using 2 forks. Use the spicy shredded beef as a filling for burritos or enchiladas.

Serves 4

Ham Meat Loaf

MEAT LOAF
2 pounds cured ham, ground
2 pounds ground beef
2 eggs

2 cups finely ground graham cracker
    crumbs
1/2 cup milk

SAUCE
1 cup tomato sauce
1/2 cup white vinegar

1 1/2 cups packed brown sugar
1 1/2 tablespoons dry mustard

For the meat loaf, combine the ground ham and ground beef in a mixing bowl and beat with the paddle attachment until well mixed. Add the eggs, cracker crumbs and milk and mix well. Pat the meat mixture into a 9×13-inch baking dish. Score the meat with a knife, cutting halfway through into serving-size pieces.

For the sauce, combine all the ingredients in a saucepan. Bring to a boil and boil until the sugar dissolves, stirring constantly. Bake the meat loaf at 350 degrees for 1 hour or until the ground meat is cooked through, basting with the sauce every 15 minutes.

Serves 16

HINT—This dish tastes even better if baked a day in advance and reheated before serving.

Mexican Lasagna

1 1/2 pounds ground beef
1 teaspoon seasoned salt
1/2 envelope taco seasoning mix
1 (15-ounce) can diced tomatoes
2 (8-ounce) cans tomato sauce
1 (4-ounce) can diced green chiles

8 ounces ricotta cheese
2 eggs
9 corn tortillas, halved
2 1/2 cups (10 ounces) shredded
    Monterey Jack cheese

Brown the ground beef in a skillet, stirring until crumbly; drain. Add the seasoned salt, taco seasoning mix, undrained tomatoes, tomato sauce and undrained green chiles. Simmer for 4 minutes, stirring occasionally. Combine the ricotta cheese and eggs in a bowl and mix well. Layer the meat sauce, tortillas, ricotta cheese mixture and Monterey Jack cheese 1/3 at a time in a 9×13-inch baking dish. Bake at 350 degrees for 20 minutes. Let stand for 10 minutes before serving.

Serves 8

Sweet-and-Sour Meatballs

2 pounds ground beef
1 cup crushed saltine crackers
1 cup milk
1 tablespoon minced onion
1 teaspoon salt

1/4 teaspoon pepper
1/3 cup vinegar
1 cup ketchup
3/4 cup packed brown sugar

Combine the ground beef, crushed crackers, milk, onion, salt and pepper in a bowl and mix well. Shape the mixture into 30 meatballs. Place in a 9×13-inch baking dish. Combine the vinegar, ketchup and brown sugar in a bowl and mix well. Pour over the meatballs. Bake, covered, at 350 degrees for 50 minutes. Bake, uncovered, for 10 minutes longer or until the ground beef is cooked through.

Serves 6

HINT—When making meatballs, use ground beef with some fat; they will stick together better and have more flavor. Meatballs will keep well in the freezer.

Three-Meat Mostaccioli

1/2 pound ground beef

3 slices bacon, chopped

1/2 pound ground pork

1/2 cup sliced fresh mushrooms or canned sliced mushrooms

1 onion, chopped

1 (32-ounce) bottle tomato juice

1 bay leaf

1/2 teaspoon basil

Salt and pepper to taste

1 tablespoon dry sherry

1 (6-ounce) can tomato paste

16 ounces mostaccioli, cooked and drained

Grated Parmesan cheese to taste

Brown the ground beef, bacon and ground pork in a large saucepan, stirring until the ground beef and ground pork are crumbly; drain. Add the mushrooms and onion and sauté until the onion is translucent. Add the tomato juice, bay leaf and basil. Season with salt and pepper. Simmer for 1 hour, stirring occasionally. Add the sherry and tomato paste and simmer for 15 minutes. Discard the bay leaf. Serve the meat sauce over the mostaccioli. Sprinkle with Parmesan cheese.

Serves 6

Cracklin' Pork

5 pounds pork loin, trimmed
1 tablespoon salt
1 teaspoon pepper

12 bay leaves
4 cups (1 quart) boiling water

Coat the pork with the salt and pepper. Cut 12 slits along the top of the pork. Insert the bay leaves into the slits halfway. Place the pork in a roasting pan. Roast at 450 degrees for 30 minutes. Add the boiling water to the pan. Reduce the oven temperature to 350 degrees and roast for 1 hour or until a meat thermometer inserted into the thickest portion of the pork registers 160 degrees. Remove the bay leaves. Let the pork stand for 10 minutes before carving.

Serves 8

Red Onion Marmalade

1/4 cup (1/2 stick) unsalted butter
1/2 cup sugar
1 1/2 pounds red onions, finely chopped
2/3 cup dry red wine

1/3 cup plus 1 tablespoon white wine
    vinegar
3 tablespoons crème de cassis

Combine the butter and sugar in a non-reactive 3-quart saucepan. Cook over low heat until the sugar dissolves, stirring frequently. Add the red onions. Cook, covered, for 30 minutes or until the onions are very soft. Stir in the wine, vinegar and crème de cassis. Increase the heat to medium and bring to a boil. Reduce the heat to low and simmer for 30 minutes, stirring occasionally. Increase the heat to high and boil for 5 minutes or until thick, stirring constantly. Remove from the heat and cool to room temperature. This recipe is great served with either beef or pork.

Serves 12

Asian Ribs

4 pounds spareribs, cut into individual ribs
2 tablespoons vinegar
3/4 cup soy sauce
2 cups pineapple juice
1 tablespoon dry mustard
2 teaspoons minced gingerroot
1 tablespoon sesame seeds

Combine the ribs with water to cover in a large stockpot. Bring to a boil and boil for 30 minutes. Pour off all but 1 1/2 cups of the cooking liquid. Add the vinegar, soy sauce, pineapple juice, dry mustard, gingerroot and sesame seeds. Simmer until thickened.

Serves 4

Pork Loin Cubano

4 cups orange juice
2 cups lemon juice
1 onion, chopped
1 cup olive oil
1 (8- to 10-pound) pork loin, trimmed
15 garlic cloves
2 tablespoons oregano

Combine the orange juice, lemon juice, onion and olive oil in a large glass dish and mix well. Add the pork loin and marinate, covered, in the refrigerator for 24 hours, turning once. Drain the pork, reserving 1 cup of the marinade. Place the reserved marinade in a small saucepan. Bring to a boil and boil for 2 to 3 minutes, stirring constantly. Mince the garlic and oregano in a food processor by pulsing 4 or 5 times. Rub the pork loin with the garlic mixture and place in a roasting pan. Pour the reserved marinade over the pork. Roast at 350 degrees until a meat thermometer inserted into the thickest portion of the pork registers 160 degrees. Let the pork stand for 10 minutes before carving.

Serves 12 to 14

Pork Roast with Sweet Potatoes and Apples

1 (2½- to 3-pound) pork roast, trimmed
Salt and pepper to taste
2 teaspoons canola oil
⅓ cup honey
¼ cup orange juice
½ cup apple juice concentrate
2 tablespoons brown sugar
1 teaspoon chicken bouillon granules
2 sweet potatoes, peeled and halved
2 Granny Smith apples, quartered and sliced

Season the pork roast with salt and pepper. Heat the canola oil in a medium roasting pan over medium-high heat. Add the pork and brown on all sides. Remove the pork to a platter. Combine the honey, orange juice, apple juice concentrate, brown sugar and bouillon granules in a bowl and mix well. Pour the honey mixture into the pan and scrape up any browned bits in the pan. Return the pork to the pan. Add the sweet potatoes.

Roast, covered, at 375 degrees for 1½ to 2 hours or until the pork is cooked through. Remove the pork and sweet potatoes and let stand for 10 minutes before carving. Add the apples to the pan. Cook over high heat until the apples are tender and the liquid is reduced and thickened. Slice the pork and serve with the sweet potatoes, apples and pan juices.

Serves 6 to 8

Chicken Cordon Bleu

2 whole chicken breasts, boned and skinned
1 teaspoon salt
1/4 teaspoon pepper
4 slices Swiss cheese
4 slices cooked ham, 1/8 inch thick
2 eggs, beaten
1 tablespoon water
6 tablespoons flour
6 tablespoons dry bread crumbs
1/4 cup (1/2 stick) butter

Pound the chicken 1/4 inch thick between sheets of waxed paper. Cut each piece in half crosswise. Season with the salt and pepper. Top with 1 slice of cheese and 1 slice of ham and roll up, securing with a wooden pick. Combine the eggs and water in a shallow bowl and mix well. Dip the chicken in the egg mixture and coat with the flour. Dip in the egg mixture again and roll in the bread crumbs. Melt the butter in a shallow baking dish. Place the chicken in the baking dish. Bake at 350 degrees for 20 minutes or until the chicken is light brown and cooked through.

Serves 4

HINT—To thaw frozen chicken for a recipe, place it in the refrigerator or defrost on Medium-Low in the microwave.

Chicken Marsala

2 tablespoons butter
1 tablespoon olive oil
4 boneless skinless chicken breasts
4 slices mozzarella cheese
12 capers
4 flat anchovies
Chopped fresh parsley to taste
1 garlic clove, minced
3 tablespoons marsala
2/3 cup heavy cream

Heat the butter and olive oil in a saucepan. Add the chicken and cook for 5 to 6 minutes per side or until firm and cooked through. Remove the chicken. Top each chicken piece with 1 slice of cheese, 3 capers and 1 anchovy. Return the chicken to the pan. Sprinkle with parsley. Cook, covered, for 3 minutes or until the cheese melts. Remove the chicken to a serving platter. Combine the garlic, wine and cream in a saucepan. Cook over medium heat until thickened, stirring frequently. Spoon the sauce over the chicken.

Serves 4

Tropical Chicken

2 (3-pound) chickens, cut up
1/2 cup flour
1 teaspoon salt
1/2 cup soy sauce
1/2 cup packed brown sugar
1/2 cup orange juice
1 (20-ounce) can crushed pineapple

Coat the chicken with flour and salt. Place the chicken in a 9×13-inch baking dish. Combine the soy sauce, brown sugar, orange juice and crushed pineapple in a bowl and mix well. Pour over the chicken. Bake, covered, at 350 degrees for 1 1/2 hours, turning the chicken over once.

Serves 6 to 8

HINT—This dish goes nicely with white rice. If dinner must wait, you can keep cooked rice hot and fluffy by placing a slice of bread on top of the rice and covering with a lid.

Pecan Chicken

$1/2$ cup (1 stick) butter or margarine
1 cup buttermilk
1 egg, slightly beaten
1 cup flour
1 cup ground pecans
1 tablespoon paprika
1 teaspoon salt
$1/8$ teaspoon pepper
$1/4$ cup sesame seeds
2 (3-pound) chickens, cut up or 6 pounds of favorite chicken parts
$1/4$ cup pecan halves

Melt the butter in a 9×13-inch baking dish. Combine the buttermilk and egg in a shallow dish and mix well. Stir the flour, ground pecans, paprika, salt, pepper and sesame seeds together in a shallow dish. Dip the chicken into the buttermilk mixture. Roll in the flour mixture, coating well. Place the chicken skin-side down in the baking dish, turning to coat with the butter. Sprinkle the pecan halves around the chicken. Bake at 350 degrees for $1^3/4$ hours. Serve with cherry tomatoes and fresh parsley.

Serves 6 to 8

HINT—To crush nuts quickly and easily, place the nuts in a sealable plastic bag. Crush the nuts with a rolling pin to the desired consistency.

Baked Chicken Soufflé

8 or 9 slices white bread, crusts trimmed
4 cups chopped cooked chicken
1/2 teaspoon poultry seasoning
1 (4- or 6-ounce) can sliced mushrooms, drained
1 (8-ounce) can sliced water chestnuts, drained and rinsed
1/2 cup mayonnaise
6 slices Old English Deluxe processed cheese
4 eggs, well beaten
2 cups milk
1/2 teaspoon salt
1 (10-ounce) can cream of mushroom soup
1 (10-ounce) can cream of celery soup
1 (2-ounce) jar chopped pimento, drained
1/2 cup buttered bread crumbs

Line a buttered 9×13-inch glass baking dish with the bread slices, completely covering the bottom. Top with the chicken and sprinkle with the poultry seasoning. Spoon the mushrooms and water chestnuts over the chicken. Dot with the mayonnaise. Top with the cheese slices. Combine the eggs, milk and salt in a bowl and mix well. Pour the egg mixture over the cheese. Stir the mushroom soup and celery soup together in a bowl. Add the pimento. Spoon the soup mixture over the prepared layers. Chill, covered with foil, for 8 hours. Do not preheat the oven. Bake the chicken at 325 degrees for 1 hour. Remove the foil, sprinkle with the bread crumbs and bake, uncovered, for 30 minutes. Let stand for 5 minutes before slicing.

Serves 12

Overnight Chicken Bake

2 cups chopped cooked chicken

2 (10-ounce) cans cream of mushroom soup

1 (14-ounce) can chicken broth

1/2 green bell pepper, finely chopped

1 (8-ounce) can water chestnuts, drained and finely chopped

2 cups (8 ounces) shredded Cheddar cheese

2 cups uncooked elbow macaroni

1 cup milk

1 small onion, finely chopped

1 (2-ounce) jar chopped pimento

Combine the chicken, mushroom soup, chicken broth, bell pepper, water chestnuts, cheese, macaroni, milk, onion and undrained pimento in a large bowl and mix well. Pour into a well-greased 9×13-inch baking dish. Chill, covered with foil, for 8 hours. Remove the foil and bake at 350 degrees for 1 hour.

Serves 8 to 10

Slow-Cooker Chicken Stew

6 cups water

1 1/2 pounds boneless skinless chicken,
  cut into bite-size pieces

3 cups chopped red potatoes

1 (10-ounce) can diced tomatoes with
  green chiles

1 1/2 cups chopped onions

1 1/2 cups frozen whole kernel corn

2 (4-ounce) cans diced green chiles

1 cup mild salsa

1 cup sliced carrots

2 tablespoons chicken bouillon granules

2 teaspoons minced fresh cilantro

2 teaspoons paprika

2 bay leaves

1 teaspoon garlic salt

1/2 teaspoon cumin

1/2 teaspoon pepper

1/2 cup evaporated milk

6 tablespoons sour cream

6 tablespoons shredded Cheddar
  cheese

6 tablespoons chopped green onions

Combine the water, chicken, potatoes, undrained tomatoes with green chiles, onions, corn, undrained green chiles, salsa, carrots, bouillon granules, cilantro, paprika, bay leaves, garlic salt, cumin and pepper in a slow cooker. Cook on Low for 8 to 10 hours or on High for 4 to 5 hours or until the chicken is tender and cooked through. Discard the bay leaves. Stir in the evaporated milk. Serve topped with the sour cream, cheese and green onions.

Serves 6

Lobster Tetrazzini

2$1/2$ cups water
2 chicken bouillon cubes
8 ounces spaghetti
1 (10-ounce) can white sauce
$1/2$ teaspoon salt
$1/4$ teaspoon pepper
1$1/2$ cups sour cream
1 cup cottage cheese
1 teaspoon minced onion
8 ounces fresh mushrooms, sliced
2 or 3 lobster tails
$1/2$ pound shrimp, peeled and deveined
1 cup (4 ounces) shredded Cheddar cheese
1 cup buttered bread crumbs

Combine the water and bouillon cubes in a large stockpot. Add the pasta and cook using the package directions until tender, being careful not to let all of the liquid evaporate. Do not drain. Remove from the heat. Combine the white sauce, salt, pepper, sour cream, cottage cheese, onion and mushrooms in a large bowl and mix well. Cut the lobster and shrimp into bite-size pieces and add to the white sauce mixture. Add the pasta and mix well. Pour the lobster mixture into a greased 2-quart baking dish. Top with the Cheddar cheese and sprinkle with the bread crumbs. Bake at 350 degrees for 45 minutes.

Serves 6 to 8

HINT—Fresh or frozen seafood may be used for this recipe. It is not necessary to cook the lobster or shrimp first.

Fettuccini with Shrimp, Tomatoes, and Basil

16 ounces fettuccini
1/4 cup olive oil
1 pound fresh shrimp, peeled and deveined
4 large tomatoes, coarsely chopped
1/2 cup chopped fresh basil
1/3 cup sliced black olives
3 large garlic cloves, minced
2 tablespoons minced green onions
Salt and pepper to taste
Grated Romano cheese to taste

Cook the pasta using the package directions until al dente; drain. Heat the olive oil in a large heavy skillet over medium heat. Add the shrimp, tomatoes, basil, olives, garlic and green onions. Cook for 3 minutes or until the shrimp turn pink. Season with salt and pepper. Toss the shrimp and pasta together and sprinkle with Romano cheese.

Serves 4

HINT—Freeze frequently used fresh herbs for up to 2 months. Store the herbs in a sealable freezer bag or plastic container. Label, date, and freeze.

Shrimp and Wild Rice Bake

3 cups cooked long grain and
    wild rice mix
2 pounds peeled cooked
    medium shrimp
1 cup (4 ounces) shredded
    longhorn cheese
1 (10-ounce) can cream of
    mushroom soup

1 tablespoon butter
1/2 cup chopped green onions
2 teaspoons Worcestershire sauce
1/2 teaspoon dry mustard
1/2 teaspoon pepper
1/4 cup milk
1 teaspoon Cajun seasoning

Combine the rice, shrimp, cheese and soup in a large bowl and mix well. Melt the butter in a large skillet. Add the green onions and cook until tender. Stir the green onions, Worcestershire sauce, dry mustard, pepper, milk and Cajun seasoning into the rice mixture and mix well. Spoon into a lightly greased 2-quart baking dish. Bake at 375 degrees for 45 minutes.

Serves 6 to 8

Spinach Cabrini

1/2 cup (1 stick) butter, melted
2 (10-ounce) packages frozen
    spinach, thawed
2 cups (8 ounces) shredded
    Monterey Jack cheese
2 cups (8 ounces) shredded
    Cheddar cheese

8 ounces sliced mushrooms
2 cups sour cream
1/4 cup chopped onion
1/4 teaspoon salt
1/4 teaspoon pepper
9 ounces spaghetti, cooked and drained

Combine the melted butter, spinach, Monterey Jack cheese, Cheddar cheese, mushrooms, sour cream, onion, salt and pepper in a large bowl and mix well. Stir in the pasta. Spoon the mixture into a 9×13-inch baking dish. Bake at 350 degrees for 45 minutes.

Serves 8 to 10

Rigatoni with Vodka Sauce

2 tablespoons olive oil
4 shallots, finely chopped
1/8 teaspoon cayenne pepper
1/2 cup vodka
3/4 cup heavy cream
3/4 cup tomato sauce
8 ounces rigatoni
4 ounces thinly sliced prosciutto, chopped
2/3 cup grated Parmesan cheese or shredded asiago cheese, divided
2 tablespoons chopped fresh parsley
2 tablespoons chopped fresh basil, or 2 teaspoons dried basil
Freshly ground pepper to taste

Heat the olive oil in a large heavy skillet over medium heat. Sauté the shallots and cayenne pepper in the hot oil for 5 minutes or until the shallots are translucent. Add the vodka. Remove from the heat and ignite with a long match. Return to the heat and simmer for 2 minutes or until the flames die, shaking the pan occasionally. Increase the heat to high. Add the cream and boil for 3 minutes or until the mixture thickens, stirring constantly. Add the tomato sauce. Boil for 2 minutes or until the sauce thickens and coats the back of a spoon.

Cook the pasta using the package directions until al dente. Drain, reserving 1/4 cup of the cooking liquid. Bring the sauce to a simmer. Add the pasta, prosciutto, 1/3 cup of the cheese, parsley and basil and toss to coat. Add the reserved cooking liquid if the sauce is too dry. Season with pepper. Remove the pasta to a large serving bowl and sprinkle with the remaining 1/3 cup cheese.

Serves 2 to 3

HINT—To prepare pasta ahead of time, cook according to the package directions, drain in a colander, rinse with cold water, and toss with a little olive oil. Store in a sealable plastic bag at room temperature for up to 2 hours.

Tortellini with Bacon and Peas

16 ounces fresh or frozen cheese tortellini
1 tablespoon safflower oil or corn oil
1/2 pound bacon, chopped
1 1/4 cups frozen baby peas
Salt to taste
1 1/4 cups heavy cream
1/4 teaspoon nutmeg
Pepper to taste
Grated Parmesan or Romano cheese to taste

Cook the pasta in a large saucepan using the package directions until tender. Drain and return the pasta to the saucepan. Heat the safflower oil in a skillet. Add the bacon and cook over high heat for 3 minutes or until the bacon is crisp-cooked, stirring occasionally. Cook the peas in a small saucepan of boiling salted water for 2 minutes or until tender; drain. Add the bacon, peas, cream, nutmeg, salt and pepper to the tortellini. Simmer for 1 to 2 minutes or until warm. Sprinkle with Parmesan cheese.

Serves 4

HINT—Always cover your pasta pot after adding the pasta. This will allow the water to return to a boil quickly to prevent the pasta from sticking together. Once the water has returned to a boil, remove the lid and cook using the package directions.

Nature's Abundance

Wild Game

Hunters and anglers from around the world come to South Dakota to enjoy nature and the fresh air of the great outdoors while pursuing their sport. Visitors and locals can spread out among 5 million acres of public hunting land. South Dakota boasts more than 12,000 camping and picnic sites, a dozen state parks, fifty recreation areas, and three state nature areas.

South Dakota has a variety of wild game. The Chinese Ringnecked Pheasant, our state bird, is the most popular among hunters. Each fall, thousands of hunters travel to our state to experience the incomparable upland bird hunting. From the expansive cornfields of eastern South Dakota to the bluffs of the Missouri River, hunters enjoy the largest number of pheasants in the nation. Duck, geese, turkey, quail, mourning dove, grouse, partridge, deer, elk, antelope, mountain goats, and big horn sheep also fill the plains, prairies, and hills of our state.

With some of the finest waters in North America, fishing enthusiasts can catch nearly thirty species of fish in the streams of the Black Hills and in the glacial lakes of eastern South Dakota. The most popular fish include walleye, salmon, bluegill, crappie, perch, bass, pike, trout, and catfish. Anglers may fish throughout all four seasons in our state.

South Dakota has been blessed with an abundance of wildlife, hunting and fishing spots, and recreational areas. From nature to the table, your taste buds will savor the unique flavors of the wild game and fish recipes in this chapter.

Venison Paprika

1/2 cup flour
Salt and pepper to taste
3 pounds venison steak, cut into 1-inch pieces
6 tablespoons butter
2 large onions, finely chopped
2 garlic cloves, minced
1 teaspoon marjoram
1 cup chopped tomato
1/4 cup dry sherry
2 tablespoons paprika
1 cup sour cream

Combine the flour, salt and pepper in a paper bag and shake to mix. Add the venison in batches and shake to coat. Melt the butter in a hot skillet. Add the venison and cook until brown. Remove to a platter.

Combine the onions, garlic, marjoram, tomato, sherry and paprika in the skillet. Cook, covered, over low heat for 15 minutes. Add the venison to the skillet and simmer, covered, for 1 hour or until tender. Stir in the sour cream. Serve the venison with cooked rice or potatoes.

Serves 6

HINT—The term venison applies to deer, elk, moose, caribou, and reindeer meat for cooking. The meats can be used interchangeably. The venison found in South Dakota are white-tailed deer, mule deer, and elk. Venison is very lean, and it is important to not overcook it. Beef may be substituted for venison in any recipe.

Grilled Venison Quesadillas

TEQUILA MARINADE
$1/3$ cup tequila
2 tablespoons olive oil
2 teaspoons chili powder
1 garlic clove, chopped
Juice of 1 lime
$1/2$ teaspoon cumin
$1/4$ teaspoon salt
$1/4$ teaspoon pepper

QUESADILLAS
$1/2$ pound venison loin steak
1 jalapeño chile
2 green bell peppers
8 (6-inch) flour tortillas
2 cups (8 ounces) shredded Monterey Jack cheese
$1/2$ cup chopped fresh cilantro

For the marinade, combine the tequila, olive oil, chili powder, garlic, lime juice, cumin, salt and pepper in a plastic container and mix well.

For the quesadillas, add the venison to the marinade. Marinate, covered, in the refrigerator for 1 hour, turning twice. Grill the jalapeño chile and bell peppers over hot coals until blackened, turning occasionally. Remove from the grill and place in a paper bag for 10 minutes. Peel the jalapeño chile and bell peppers under running water. Seed the jalapeño chile and bell peppers and cut into thin strips; set aside. Grill the venison over hot coals to medium doneness. Thinly slice the venison across the grain.

Place 4 tortillas on a baking sheet. Top with $1/2$ of the cheese, the venison, jalapeño chile, bell peppers, cilantro and the remaining 1 cup cheese. Top with the remaining 4 tortillas. Grill over hot coals until the quesadillas are golden brown on both sides and the cheese is melted, turning once. Cut the quesadillas into wedges and serve.

Serves 8

Venison Finger Steaks

$1/3$ cup Dijon mustard

3 tablespoons Worcestershire sauce

$1/2$ teaspoon cayenne pepper

1 pound venison round steak

1 cup finely crushed saltine crackers

Vegetable oil for deep-frying

1 cup cocktail sauce

Combine the Dijon mustard, Worcestershire sauce and cayenne pepper in a shallow bowl and mix well. Cut the venison into $4\times1\times1/2$-inch strips. Place the crushed crackers in a shallow dish. Dip the venison into the Dijon mustard sauce and dredge in the crackers. Heat the oil in a deep-fat fryer or 12-inch skillet to medium-hot. Add half the venison and cook for 4 to 5 minutes or until golden brown; drain. Fry the remaining venison. Serve with the cocktail sauce.

Serves 4

Barbecued Venison Meatballs

$1^1/2$ pounds ground venison

$1/2$ pound ground beef

2 slices dry bread, soaked in milk

1 egg, beaten

Garlic salt to taste

Salt and pepper to taste

$1/4$ cup minced green onions, green
   parts only

$1/4$ cup minced fresh parsley

1 white onion, chopped

2 ribs celery, chopped

Vegetable oil

1 cup barbecue sauce

1 (10-ounce) can cream of mushroom
   soup

Combine the ground venison, ground beef, bread, egg, garlic salt, salt, pepper, green onions, parsley, white onion and celery in a bowl and mix well. Shape into 1-inch balls or bite-size balls. Heat a small amount of oil in a large skillet. Brown the meatballs on all sides in the skillet; drain. Remove the meatballs to a serving dish. Combine the barbecue sauce and soup in the skillet and heat. Pour the barbecue sauce mixture over the meatballs.

Makes 24 dinner-size meatballs or 125 bite-size meatballs

HINT—To serve as appetizers, keep the meatballs warm in a chafing dish or slow cooker.

Dove Breast Rumaki Hors d'Oeuvre

3 whole dove breasts
6 slices bacon, halved
1/2 cup baking mix
3 pineapple rings, quartered into
    1-inch pieces

12 macadamia nut halves
Sweet-and-sour sauce

Bone the dove breasts and cut each breast into 4 pieces. Dredge the bacon slices in the baking mix. Place 1 pineapple piece on each bacon strip. Add 1 macadamia nut half and 1 dove piece. Roll up the bacon strip and secure with a wooden pick. Arrange the rumaki on a greased baking sheet, being careful so they are not touching. Bake at 400 degrees for 30 to 45 minutes or until the bacon is brown and crisp and the dove is cooked through, turning frequently. Serve with sweet-and-sour sauce for dipping.

Serves 4

Grilled Breast of Mallard

1/3 cup soy sauce
1/3 cup sesame oil
1/4 cup olive oil
1/2 teaspoon garlic powder
2 teaspoons fresh fennel, or
    1/2 teaspoon dried fennel

2 teaspoons fresh tarragon, or
    1/2 teaspoon dried tarragon
Mongolian Fire Oil
4 to 6 Mallard duck breast halves

Combine the soy sauce, sesame oil, olive oil, garlic powder, fennel and tarragon in a sealable plastic bag. Add 2 dashes of Mongolian Fire Oil for each duck breast half. Add the duck and seal the bag. Marinate for 4 to 8 hours in the refrigerator, turning occasionally. Drain the duck and discard the marinade. Grill the duck over hot coals for 3 to 5 minutes per side or until cooked through. Do not overcook the duck or it will be tough.

Serves 4 to 6

HINT—Always use tongs or a spatula to turn meat when grilling. Piercing the meat with a fork not only dries the meat by allowing the juices to escape, but it may also introduce bacteria into the center of the meat and contaminate it.

Duck Gumbo

1 domestic duck, or 3 or 4 wild duck
1 cup vegetable oil
1 cup flour
1^1/$_2$ cups chopped onions
1 cup chopped celery
2 garlic cloves, minced
1 tablespoon butter
^{1}/$_2$ (10-ounce) package frozen okra, thawed
Filé powder to taste
Salt and pepper to taste
Tabasco sauce to taste
Hot cooked rice

Combine the duck with water to cover in a large stockpot. Bring to a boil and boil for 1 hour. Remove the duck and reserve the broth. Chill the broth, covered, until the fat solidifies. Discard the fat. Reheat the broth over low heat. Cut the duck into bite-size pieces and add to the broth.

Heat the oil in a large iron saucepan. Add the flour and cook over low heat for 20 to 30 minutes or until the mixture is a rich chocolate color and begins to separate, stirring constantly. Add the onions, celery and garlic and cook until the onions are translucent. Add the duck and broth. Simmer until the liquid is reduced by ^{1}/$_3$. Heat the butter in a saucepan. Add the okra and briefly sauté over high heat. Add the okra to the gumbo just before serving. Season with filé powder, salt, pepper and Tabasco sauce. Serve over cooked rice.

Serves 12

Goose Stroganoff

2 pounds boneless skinless goose breast, chopped
3/4 cup water
3/4 cup minced onion or dried onion flakes
1/4 teaspoon salt
1/4 teaspoon pepper
2 (10-ounce) cans cream of chicken soup
1/2 cup sour cream
Hot cooked rice, mashed potatoes, noodles or toast

Combine the goose and water in a 9×13-inch baking dish. Sprinkle with the onion, salt and pepper. Bake, covered with foil, at 325 degrees for 2 hours. Combine the soup and sour cream in a bowl and mix well. Add the soup mixture to the goose and mix well. Bake at 325 degrees for 30 minutes. Serve the goose over cooked rice, mashed potatoes, noodles or toast.

Serves 8

HINT—When slicing or chopping meats or poultry, it is much easier if the meat is partially frozen. If using fresh meat, place it in the freezer for 30 to 45 minutes or until very firm, then slice.

Pheasant Pierre

3/4 cup flour
Salt and pepper to taste
2 pheasants, grouse or prairie chickens, quartered
1 cup olive oil
2 garlic cloves, halved
1 cup white wine
1 cup red wine
1/4 teaspoon dried basil, or 1 teaspoon fresh basil
2 shallots, or 1 onion, minced
1 cup sliced mushrooms
1 or 2 tomatoes, sliced
1 cup sour cream

Combine the flour, salt and pepper in a paper bag and shake to mix. Add the pheasant pieces 1 at a time and shake to coat. Heat the olive oil in a large skillet. Add the garlic and brown; discard the garlic. Brown the pheasant pieces in the hot oil; drain. Remove 1/4 cup of the oil to a baking dish. Spoon the pheasant into the prepared baking dish. Add the white wine and red wine. Sprinkle with the basil, shallots and mushrooms. Top with the tomato slices. Season with salt and pepper. Bake, covered, at 350 degrees for 11/2 hours. Top with the sour cream and bake, uncovered, for 5 minutes.

Serves 6

HINT—When slicing ingredients in the kitchen, a sharp knife is of utmost importance. A dull knife requires more pressure for slicing. That could cause a slip resulting in injury. Keeping a sharp edge on a knife not only makes the tool safer but saves preparation time.

Pheasant in Cream Sauce

1 pheasant, quartered
1 (10-ounce) can cream of chicken soup
1/2 cup apple juice or apple cider
4 teaspoons Worcestershire sauce
3/4 teaspoon salt

1/3 cup chopped onion
1 garlic clove, minced
1 (4-ounce) can sliced mushrooms,
　drained
Paprika to taste

Place the pheasant in a 9×9-inch baking dish. Combine the soup, apple juice, Worcestershire sauce, salt, onion, garlic and mushrooms in a bowl and mix well. Pour the soup mixture over the pheasant. Sprinkle generously with paprika. Bake at 350 degrees for 1 1/2 to 2 hours or until fork-tender, basting occasionally with the sauce. Sprinkle the pheasant with paprika after 1 hour of baking.

Serves 2 or 3

Pheasant and Wild Rice

12 ounces bulk pork sausage
1 large onion, finely chopped
8 ounces mushrooms, sliced
1 (8-ounce) can water chestnuts,
　drained and chopped
1/2 lemon
2 (6-ounce) packages wild rice mix
1 (10-ounce) can cream of mushroom
　soup

1 (10-ounce) can cream of celery soup
1 1/4 cups milk
1 teaspoon salt
1/2 teaspoon black pepper
2 cups chopped cooked pheasant
1/2 cup slivered toasted almonds
1/2 cup sliced almonds

Brown the sausage in a skillet, stirring until crumbly; drain. Sauté the onion and mushrooms in the skillet until tender. Add the water chestnuts when the vegetables are almost tender. Squeeze the lemon over the mushroom mixture. Prepare the wild rice mix using the package directions. Combine the mushroom soup, celery soup, milk, wild rice, salt, pepper, pheasant, sausage, mushroom mixture and toasted almonds in a large bowl and mix well. Pour into a 9×13-inch baking pan. Sprinkle with the sliced almonds. Bake at 350 degrees for 1 hour.

Serves 10 to 12

Bacon-Wrapped Pheasant Bites

1 cup red wine
1 teaspoon horseradish
1 tablespoon soy sauce
1 tablespoon Worcestershire sauce
1 teaspoon garlic salt
1/2 teaspoon pepper
2 pheasants, boned and cut into 1-inch pieces
1/2 pound thick-sliced bacon

Whisk the red wine, horseradish, soy sauce, Worcestershire sauce, garlic salt and pepper in a large glass dish until combined. Wrap each pheasant piece with a slice of bacon and secure with a wooden pick. Add the pheasant to the marinade. Marinate, covered, in the refrigerator for 8 to 12 hours. Discard the marinade. Grill the pheasant over medium-hot coals for 10 minutes, turning frequently to prevent the bacon from burning.

Serves 8

HINT—The Chinese Ringnecked Pheasant is the state bird of South Dakota. It was introduced into our state in 1898 and is easily recognized by its colorful green head and distinctive white ring of plumage around its neck. Primarily a Midwestern bird, many other states consider its delicious meat a delicacy.

Pheasant and Poppy Seed Bake

1/4 cup (1/2 stick) butter
2 sleeves butter crackers, crumbled
1 (10-ounce) can cream of chicken
    soup
1 (10-ounce) can cream of mushroom
    soup

1 1/2 cups sour cream
2 tablespoons poppy seeds
2 pheasants, boned and cut into
    1/2-inch pieces
1/2 cup chopped celery
1/2 cup chopped onion

Melt the butter in a skillet. Add the cracker crumbs and sauté until brown. Combine the chicken soup, mushroom soup, sour cream and poppy seeds in a bowl and mix well. Place 1/2 of the cracker crumbs in a 9×13-inch baking dish. Top with the pheasant, celery and onion. Spread the soup mixture over the vegetables and sprinkle with the remaining cracker crumbs. Bake, covered, at 375 degrees for 1 1/2 hours.

Serves 8 to 10

Pheasant Consommé with Homemade Croutons

1 pheasant
10 cups (2 1/2 quarts) water
4 ribs celery with leaves
1 carrot, grated
4 leeks
2 sprigs of fresh dill weed
1 teaspoon rosemary
2 dashes of Tabasco sauce

1/2 teaspoon grated lemon zest
1 cup sliced mushrooms
1/4 cup (1/2 stick) butter
1/4 teaspoon chervil
1/8 teaspoon oregano
1/8 teaspoon thyme
2 slices white bread, cubed
Salt and pepper to taste

Combine the pheasant, water, celery, carrot, leeks, dill weed, rosemary, Tabasco sauce and lemon zest in a large pot and bring to a boil. Reduce the heat to low. Simmer, covered, for 1 hour. Remove the pheasant, carve the meat from the bird and chop into 1/2-inch pieces. Reserve the meat. Coarsely chop the carcass and return to the pot. Simmer for 1 1/2 hours. Strain through a layer of cheesecloth into a second pot. Add the reserved pheasant meat and the mushrooms.

Melt the butter in a skillet. Add the chervil, oregano and thyme. Add the bread cubes and stir to coat. Place the bread on a baking sheet. Bake at 300 degrees for 10 minutes or until golden brown. Season with salt and pepper. Ladle into heated crocks; top with the croutons.

Serves 10

Wild Rice and Pheasant Soup

2 tablespoons butter
1 bunch scallions, chopped
1/4 cup flour
4 cups chicken broth
2 cups cooked wild rice

1 pheasant, cooked and cut into
    bite-size pieces
1 teaspoon salt
1 cup heavy cream
2 tablespoons dry sherry

Melt the butter in a 3-quart saucepan. Add the scallions and sauté until tender. Add the flour. Cook for 1 minute, stirring constantly. Gradually stir in the chicken broth. Cook over medium heat until thickened, stirring constantly. Stir in the wild rice, pheasant and salt. Simmer for 5 minutes. Stir in the cream and sherry. Simmer until the soup is heated through; do not boil.

Serves 6

Fresh Citrus Turkey

2 cups Dijon mustard
1/2 cup soy sauce
Juice of 6 lemons (rinds reserved)
1/2 cup orange juice
3/4 cup olive oil

1 (15- to 20-pound) wild or fresh turkey,
    cleaned
Sprigs of rosemary, basil, sage and
    thyme to taste
Salt and pepper to taste

Whisk the Dijon mustard, soy sauce, lemon juice, orange juice and olive oil in a large glass dish until blended. Add the turkey. Marinate, covered, in the refrigerator for 12 to 24 hours. Drain the turkey, reserving the marinade. Place the reserved marinade in a small saucepan. Bring to a boil. Boil for 2 to 3 minutes, stirring constantly.

Stuff the turkey with rosemary, basil, sage and thyme sprigs and the reserved lemon rinds. Season with salt and pepper. Place on a rack in a roasting pan. Cover with foil. Roast at 400 degrees for 1 1/2 hours. Remove the foil. Roast for 2 1/2 to 3 hours or until a meat thermometer inserted into the thickest portion of the turkey registers 180 degrees, basting every 15 minutes with the reserved marinade. Let stand for 30 minutes before carving.

Serves 10

Midwest Pâté

3 pounds turkey drumsticks or duck or
    goose meat
Water or broth
4 shallots, chopped
2 garlic cloves
1/4 teaspoon allspice
1 teaspoon minced fresh marjoram, or
    1/2 teaspoon dried marjoram
2 teaspoons minced fresh thyme, or
    1 teaspoon dried thyme
1/4 teaspoon mace
2 tablespoons brandy
1 cup heavy cream
1/4 teaspoon salt
1/4 teaspoon pepper

Combine the turkey with water to cover in a large stockpot. Simmer for 1 1/2 hours or until the turkey is tender and cooked through. Remove the turkey from the drumsticks; discard the skin and bones. Place the turkey, shallots, garlic, allspice, marjoram, thyme, mace and brandy in a food processor and process for 1 minute. Slowly add the cream while continuously processing. Stir in the salt and pepper. Spoon the pâté into a ceramic or glass container and chill, covered, for 8 hours. Serve with toasted baguette slices or crackers.

Makes 3 cups

Wild Turkey Kabobs

1/3 cup vegetable oil
1/2 cup cooking sherry
1/2 cup soy sauce
1 teaspoon ginger
1 teaspoon garlic salt
1/3 cup sugar or packed brown sugar
2 (20-ounce) cans pineapple chunks
Boneless wild turkey, cut into 1-inch pieces
Cherry tomatoes
Mushrooms

Whisk the oil, sherry, soy sauce, ginger, garlic salt and sugar in a glass dish until combined. Drain the pineapple, reserving the juice. Place the pineapple chunks in a container and chill, covered, in the refrigerator. Add the reserved juice to the marinade and whisk well. Add the turkey. Marinate, covered, in the refrigerator for 4 to 24 hours. Drain the turkey, reserving the marinade. Place the reserved marinade in a small saucepan. Bring to a boil. Boil for 2 to 3 minutes, stirring constantly.

Thread the turkey pieces, pineapple chunks, cherry tomatoes and mushrooms onto wooden skewers. Grill over hot coals for 15 to 20 minutes or until the turkey and vegetables are cooked through, turning frequently and basting with the reserved marinade.

Variable servings

HINT—Before assembling the kabobs for the grill, soak the wooden skewers in water to prevent them from burning.

Catfish Pinwheels with Mushroom Sauce

PINWHEELS

2 tablespoons butter	1/2 teaspoon salt
1/2 cup chopped fresh mushrooms	1/8 teaspoon pepper
2 tablespoons finely chopped celery	1/8 teaspoon ground sage
2 tablespoons finely chopped onion	4 skinless catfish, Northern pike or
1/2 cup herb-seasoned stuffing mix	walleye pike fillets
2 tablespoons hot water	1 tablespoon butter, melted

MUSHROOM SAUCE

2 tablespoons butter	1/8 teaspoon pepper
2 cups chopped fresh mushrooms	1/3 cup milk
1/4 cup chopped onion	1/4 cup sour cream
1 tablespoon flour	1 tablespoon Dijon mustard
1/4 teaspoon salt	1 tablespoon white wine

For the pinwheels, melt the butter in a small skillet. Add the mushrooms, celery and onion and cook over medium heat for 4 minutes or until the onion is tender, stirring frequently. Remove from the heat. Add the stuffing mix, hot water, salt, pepper and sage and stir until the mixture is moistened. Spread 1/4 of the stuffing mixture over each fillet. Roll to enclose the filling, starting at the narrow end. Arrange the pinwheels upright in a staggered pattern in a greased loaf pan. Brush with the melted butter. Bake, covered, at 375 degrees for 30 to 35 minutes or until the fish flake easily.

For the sauce, melt the butter in a small saucepan or skillet. Add the mushrooms and onion and cook over medium heat for 5 minutes or until the onion is tender, stirring frequently. Stir in the flour, salt and pepper. Blend in the milk. Cook over medium heat for 3 minutes or until thickened, stirring constantly. Remove from the heat. Stir in the sour cream, Dijon mustard and wine. Serve the sauce with the fish.

Serves 4

Salmon Loaf with Mushroom and Spinach Stuffing

SALMON LOAF

2 cups flaked cooked salmon, cooking liquid reserved, or 1 (15-ounce) can salmon, liquid reserved

2 cups soft bread crumbs

2 eggs, beaten

1 tablespoon lemon juice

1 tablespoon finely chopped onion

1/2 teaspoon salt

2 tablespoons butter

1 1/2 cups sliced mushrooms

1 cup fresh spinach, cut into thin strips

LEMON BUTTER SAUCE

Reserved salmon liquid

Milk

1 tablespoon butter

1 tablespoon flour

1/8 teaspoon salt

Dash of pepper

1 egg yolk

1 tablespoon lemon juice

For the salmon loaf, combine the salmon, bread crumbs, eggs, lemon juice, onion and salt in a bowl and mix well. Pat 1/2 of the salmon mixture into a greased 4×8-inch loaf pan. Melt the butter in a skillet. Add the mushrooms and sauté for 1 minute. Add the spinach and sauté until wilted. Spread the mushroom mixture over the salmon, leaving a 1-inch border. Top with the remaining salmon mixture. Bake at 350 degrees for 40 minutes or until the loaf is puffed, set and golden brown.

For the lemon butter sauce, combine the reserved salmon liquid with enough milk to measure 2/3 cup in a measuring cup. Melt the butter in a small saucepan. Stir in the flour, salt and pepper. Whisk in the milk mixture. Cook until thickened, stirring constantly. Beat the egg yolk in a heatproof bowl. Pour a little of the sauce into the egg yolk, stirring constantly. Pour the egg yolk into the pan. Cook over low heat until thickened, stirring constantly. Stir in the lemon juice. Serve the salmon loaf with the lemon butter sauce.

Serves 6

Sesame and Dill Broiled Salmon

3 tablespoons butter
1 tablespoon sesame seeds
1 teaspoon dill weed
1/4 teaspoon salt
1/8 teaspoon pepper
4 salmon steaks, 1 inch thick

Melt the butter in a small skillet over medium heat. Add the sesame seeds and dill weed and cook for 4 minutes or until the sesame seeds are light brown. Stir in the salt and pepper. Remove from the heat. Place the salmon on a greased rack in a broiler pan. Brush with 1/2 of the sesame seed mixture. Broil the salmon 5 to 6 inches from the heat source for 5 minutes. Turn the fish and brush with the remaining sesame seed mixture. Broil for 5 minutes longer or until the fish flake easily in the center.

Serves 4

Walleye with Grapes

1 cup flour
4 to 6 medium walleye pike fillets (1 to 11/2 pounds)
Salt to taste
Nutmeg to taste
3 tablespoons butter, divided
1 cup seedless green grapes, halved
1/2 cup heavy cream

Place the flour in a shallow bowl and dredge the fish, shaking off any excess flour. Season the fish lightly with salt and sprinkle with nutmeg. Melt 2 tablespoons of the butter in a skillet over medium heat. Add the fish. Cook until golden brown on both sides, turning once. Remove the fish to a serving dish and keep hot. Add the remaining 1 tablespoon butter to the pan. Add the grapes. Swirl over high heat until the grapes are warm and bright green. Pour the grapes over the fish. Pour the cream into the pan and bring to a boil. Cook the cream over high heat until golden brown, stirring constantly. Drizzle the cream over the fish.

Serves 4

Crunchy Coated Walleye

$1/3$ cup flour

1 teaspoon paprika

$1/2$ teaspoon salt

$1/4$ teaspoon pepper

$1/4$ teaspoon onion powder

$1/4$ teaspoon garlic powder

2 eggs

$21/4$ pounds walleye pike fillets

$11/2$ cups instant mashed potato flakes

$1/3$ cup vegetable oil

Combine the flour, paprika, salt, pepper, onion powder and garlic powder in a shallow bowl. Beat the eggs in a shallow bowl. Coat each fish fillet in the flour mixture, then in the eggs, then with the mashed potato flakes. Heat the oil in a large skillet. Add the fish and fry for 5 minutes per side or until the fish flake easily. Serve with tartar sauce and lemon wedges.

Serves 4

HINT—To cut down on the fishy flavor of frozen fillets, thaw the fillets immersed in milk. When calculating the cooking time of fish fillets, measure the thickest part of the fillet and gauge 10 minutes of cooking per inch of fillet.

Walleye Cakes with Blue Cheese Aïoli Sauce

FISH CAKES

8 ounces walleye pike fillet

1 1/2 cups mayonnaise

1 cup cooked wild rice

4 green onions, finely chopped

1 garlic clove, minced

1/2 cup (2 ounces) grated Parmesan cheese

4 eggs

2 teaspoons seasonings, such as parsley, oregano, basil, rosemary or pepper

1 sleeve saltine crackers, crushed

2 tablespoons vegetable oil or butter

AÏOLI SAUCE

1/2 cup mayonnaise

1 garlic clove, minced

1 ounce blue cheese, crumbled

For the fish cakes, cook the walleye in simmering water in a saucepan for 5 minutes or until the fish is firm; drain. Let stand until cool. Flake the walleye using a fork. Combine the walleye, mayonnaise, wild rice, green onions, garlic and cheese in a bowl and mix well. Add the eggs and mix with a fork. Add the parsley. Add the cracker crumbs and mix well. Form the fish mixture into cakes using a 1/3-cup measure. Heat the oil in a skillet over medium-high heat. Cook the fish cakes in the hot oil for 2 to 3 minutes per side or until golden brown.

For the aïoli sauce, combine the mayonnaise, garlic and blue cheese in a bowl and mix well. Serve the fish cakes with the aïoli sauce.

Serves 4 to 5

HINT—The walleye is not only our state fish, but the most sought-after game fish in South Dakota. The Glacial Lakes and Missouri River reservoirs of our state hold great numbers of this species, and for this reason, many national sportswriters have proclaimed South Dakota the "Walleye Capital" of America.

Farmer's Bounty

Vegetables and Side Dishes

South Dakota Farm • *Greg Latza, Peoplescapes Publishing*

Since early pioneer days, farming has been a way of life for many residents of South Dakota. Acres of farmland cover the rolling plains of our state, and hardworking farmers send the fruits of their labor to tables across the nation.

Agriculture is one of the leading industries in eastern South Dakota. You will find fields of corn, oats, wheat, sunflowers, rye, soybeans, alfalfa, hay, sorghum, and barley. Today there are more than 32,000 farms in South Dakota with more than 16 million acres of harvested farmland. As you travel the state, you may be surprised to find the occasional vineyard and winery.

In 1892, the world's only Corn Palace was built in Mitchell, South Dakota, to celebrate the fertile farmland and to promote settlement in our state. The exterior of the palace is decorated with 3,000 bushels of corn, grain, oats, wheat, and native grasses. Each summer, new murals are created to depict life in South Dakota. The Corn Palace stands as a tribute to the agricultural heritage of our state.

Ranching is the primary industry on the western side of the state, where herds of cattle, horses, and sheep roam the plains. Wild prairie grasses feed the cattle year-round, producing some of the world's finest meats.

The tradition of family farming in South Dakota continues today. In this chapter, you will find a recipe to accompany any meal using a medley of vegetables, whether fresh from the field or from your local grocer. These dishes will grace your table with the colors and flavors of South Dakota's bountiful farms.

Asparagus Bake

2¹/2 pounds asparagus
1 (4-ounce) jar sliced pimentos, drained (optional)
¹/2 cup milk
3 ounces cream cheese
¹/4 cup (1 ounce) crumbled blue cheese
1 teaspoon Worcestershire sauce
1 tablespoon melted butter
3 tablespoons bread crumbs
¹/4 cup (1 ounce) grated Parmesan cheese

Steam the asparagus until tender-crisp; drain. Place the asparagus in a buttered shallow baking dish. Sprinkle with the pimento. Combine the milk, cream cheese and blue cheese in a small saucepan and heat through, stirring constantly until smooth. Add the Worcestershire sauce. Pour the cheese sauce over the asparagus. Combine the butter, bread crumbs and Parmesan cheese in a bowl and mix well. Sprinkle over the cheese sauce. Bake at 325 degrees for 30 minutes.

Serves 4 to 6

HINT—Purchase asparagus with smooth stems and tightly closed tips. You may store asparagus for up to 3 days in the refrigerator with a damp paper towel wrapped around the stem ends or with the stem ends submerged in 1 inch of water. It is best to cook asparagus in a glass or enameled pan; asparagus causes metal to discolor.

Asparagus with Pistachio and Orange Glaze

2 pounds asparagus
3/4 cup (1 1/2 sticks) butter or margarine
6 tablespoons coarsely chopped
    pistachios

2 teaspoons grated orange zest
1/4 cup orange juice
1/8 teaspoon pepper

Steam the asparagus until tender-crisp; drain. Arrange the asparagus on a serving plate and keep warm. Melt the butter in a skillet over medium heat. Add the pistachios and cook for 3 to 4 minutes or until light brown. Add the orange zest and orange juice and heat through. Drizzle the pistachio mixture over the asparagus. Season with the pepper.

Serves 4 to 6

Cheese Scalloped Carrots

8 cups sliced fresh or thawed frozen
    carrots
1/4 cup (1/2 stick) margarine
1 small onion, minced
1/4 cup flour
1/4 teaspoon dry mustard
1 teaspoon salt

2 cups milk
1/8 teaspoon pepper
1/4 teaspoon celery salt
2 cups (8 ounces) shredded American
    cheese
Croutons or buttered bread crumbs

Steam the fresh carrots until tender-crisp; drain. Melt the margarine in a saucepan over medium heat. Add the onion and cook until tender. Stir in the flour, dry mustard and salt to form a paste. Add the milk. Cook until slightly thickened, stirring constantly. Season with the pepper and celery salt. Layer 1/2 of the carrots and all the cheese in a 9×13-inch baking pan. Top with the remaining carrots. Pour the white sauce over the carrots. Bake at 350 degrees for 35 minutes. Sprinkle with croutons. Bake for 10 minutes longer.

Serves 10 to 12

Roasted Cauliflower

1 head cauliflower, cut into florets
3 tablespoons olive oil
2 teaspoons seasoned salt

Place the cauliflower in a large bowl or sealable plastic bag. Add the olive oil and seasoned salt, stirring to coat. Arrange the cauliflower on a baking sheet. Roast at 400 degrees for 20 to 25 minutes or until the cauliflower begins to brown. You may prepare the cauliflower a day in advance if desired and chill, covered, until ready to bake. Bake just before serving.

Serves 6

Indian Eggplant

1 large eggplant, sliced 1/2 inch thick
2 tablespoons vegetable oil
1 small onion, chopped
1 green chile, seeded and chopped
1 tablespoon fresh lime juice
1 tablespoon garam masala (spice blend available in large grocery or specialty stores)
1/2 cup plain yogurt
3 tablespoons chopped fresh cilantro
1 teaspoon salt, or more to taste

Arrange the eggplant on a baking sheet. Bake at 350 degrees for 20 minutes. Remove from the oven and cut into 1/2-inch cubes. Heat the oil in a large sauté pan. Add the onion and green chile and sauté until the onion is translucent. Add the lime juice and garam masala and mix well. Add the eggplant to the pan. Cook for 5 to 10 minutes or until the eggplant is tender and the vegetables are hot, stirring occasionally. Stir in the yogurt, cilantro and salt. Serve the eggplant with a dollop of plain yogurt if desired.

Serves 4 to 6

Creole Corn

4 slices bacon
1/4 cup chopped onion
1/4 cup chopped green bell pepper
3/4 cup canned tomatoes, chopped
2 cups canned corn
Hot red pepper sauce or Tabasco sauce to taste

Fry the bacon in a heavy 3-quart saucepan until crisp-cooked. Remove the bacon; crumble and set aside. Pour off all but 2 tablespoons bacon drippings. Sauté the onion and bell pepper in the reserved drippings until the onion is translucent. Add the tomatoes. Simmer, covered, for 15 minutes. Stir in the corn and hot sauce. Add the bacon and cook until heated through, stirring constantly.

Serves 6

Dakota Corn Bake

1 (17-ounce) can cream-style corn
1 (16-ounce) can whole kernel corn
1 cup sour cream
1/4 cup chopped onion
1 (8-ounce) package corn muffin mix
2 eggs, beaten
1/2 cup (1 stick) butter, melted
Salt and pepper to taste
1 cup (4 ounces) shredded Cheddar cheese (optional)

Combine the cream-style corn, undrained whole kernel corn, sour cream, onion, corn muffin mix, eggs, melted butter, salt and pepper in a large bowl and mix well. Stir in the cheese. Spread the corn mixture in a greased 9×13-inch baking dish. Bake at 350 degrees for 45 minutes or until puffed and golden brown.

Serves 12

Parmesan Smashed Potatoes

3 pounds red potatoes
1 tablespoon plus 2 teaspoons kosher salt, divided
1 1/2 cups half-and-half
1/2 cup (1 stick) unsalted butter
1/2 cup sour cream
1/2 cup (2 ounces) freshly grated Parmesan cheese
1/2 teaspoon freshly ground pepper

Combine the potatoes and 1 tablespoon salt with water to cover in a saucepan. Bring to a boil. Reduce the heat and simmer, covered, for 25 to 35 minutes or until the potatoes are tender; drain. Spoon the potatoes into a large mixing bowl and mash with a fork. Combine the half-and-half and butter in a small saucepan. Heat until the butter is melted and the mixture is blended, stirring frequently. Add the half-and-half mixture to the potatoes gradually, beating constantly at low speed. Stir in the last of the half-and-half mixture by hand. Fold in the sour cream, cheese, remaining 2 teaspoons salt and the pepper. Adjust the seasonings to taste.

Serves 6 to 8

HINT—Be careful to not mix the potatoes for too long with an electric mixer. Too much mixing will release the starches in the potatoes, causing them to become rubbery, rather than fluffy.

Crispy Potato Pancakes

4 russet potatoes, peeled   3 tablespoons flour
1 tablespoon lemon juice   1 teaspoon salt
1 onion, grated   1 teaspoon pepper
4 eggs   Vegetable oil for frying

Grate the potatoes into a large bowl. Add the lemon juice, onion, eggs, flour, salt and pepper and mix well. Heat 1/8 inch of oil in a heavy skillet or electric skillet. Drop the batter by the spoonful into the hot oil and flatten into a pancake shape with the back of a spoon. Fry the pancakes for 3 to 5 minutes per side or until brown. Serve the pancakes with applesauce, sugar, sour cream or preserves.

Makes 3 dozen

Roasted New Potatoes with Prosciutto

12 new potatoes, halved lengthwise   1 tablespoon chopped fresh rosemary
Salt to taste   Olive oil for roasting
2/3 cup grated Parmesan cheese   4 slices prosciutto or bacon,
1 tablespoon chopped fresh parsley   cut into strips

Combine the potatoes with salted water to cover in a large saucepan. Bring to a boil and boil for 10 minutes; drain. Combine the cheese, parsley and rosemary in a shallow bowl. Roll the potato halves in the cheese mixture to completely coat. Pour a little olive oil into a roasting pan. Bake at 400 degrees for 10 minutes. Arrange the potatoes in the pan. Roast at 400 degrees for 30 minutes, turning once. Cover with the prosciutto strips. Roast for 5 minutes or until the potatoes are tender and the prosciutto is cooked through.

Serves 6

Praline Sweet Potatoes

SWEET POTATOES

2 pounds sweet potatoes, cooked, peeled and chopped

2 tablespoons brown sugar

2 tablespoons brandy

1 egg yolk

2 tablespoons butter, softened

1/2 teaspoon salt

1/2 teaspoon pepper

TOPPING

1/4 cup (1/2 stick) butter, softened

6 tablespoons brown sugar

2/3 cup chopped pecans

1/2 teaspoon nutmeg

For the sweet potatoes, beat the sweet potatoes in a mixing bowl until smooth. Add the brown sugar, brandy, egg yolk, butter, salt and pepper and beat until blended. Spoon the sweet potato mixture into a greased 9×9-inch baking dish.

For the topping, combine the butter, brown sugar, pecans and nutmeg in a bowl and mix by hand until crumbly. Sprinkle the pecan mixture over the sweet potatoes. Bake at 350 degrees for 30 minutes.

Serves 8

HINT—Brandy can be purchased in miniature bottles, which contain enough brandy to make this recipe twice.

Spinach Carbonara

1/4 cup chopped onion

1/4 cup sliced mushrooms

1/4 cup (1/2 stick) butter, melted

9 ounces linguini, broken into pieces, cooked and drained

2 (10-ounce) packages frozen chopped spinach, cooked and drained

4 cups (16 ounces) shredded Monterey Jack cheese

2 cups sour cream

1/4 teaspoon oregano

1/4 teaspoon salt

1/4 teaspoon pepper

Sauté the onion and mushrooms in the butter in a small skillet until tender. Combine the onion, mushrooms, pasta, spinach, cheese, sour cream, oregano, salt and pepper in a large bowl and mix well. Spoon into a greased 9×13-inch baking pan. Bake at 350 degrees for 45 minutes.

Serves 12

HINT—Use a spatula to press spinach against the sides of colander to remove excess moisture.

Spinach-Stuffed Portobello Mushrooms

2 tablespoons butter
2 tablespoons chopped onion
1 tablespoon chopped garlic
1/2 cup evaporated milk
3/4 cup chicken broth, divided
2 teaspoons Worcestershire sauce
1 tablespoon cornstarch
3 ounces cream cheese
1 (4-ounce) can diced green chiles
1 teaspoon salt
1/2 teaspoon pepper
2 (10-ounce) packages frozen chopped spinach, thawed
1/2 cup (2 ounces) grated Parmesan cheese
6 ounces sliced Swiss cheese, divided
8 small to medium portobello mushroom caps

Melt the butter in a medium saucepan. Add the onion and garlic and sauté until the onion is tender. Add the evaporated milk, 1/2 cup of the chicken broth and the Worcestershire sauce and mix well. Dissolve the cornstarch in the remaining 1/4 cup chicken broth in a small bowl. Stir into the onion mixture. Cook over low heat until thickened, stirring occasionally. Add the cream cheese, green chiles, salt and pepper. Drain the spinach, pressing out the excess moisture, and place in a large bowl. Add the onion mixture and mix well. Stir in the Parmesan cheese. Tear 1 slice of the Swiss cheese into small pieces and add to the spinach mixture. Place the mushroom caps stem side up in a shallow baking dish. Fill with the spinach mixture. Cut the remaining Swiss cheese slices into strips and place over the stuffed mushroom caps. Bake at 350 degrees for 25 to 30 minutes or until the mushrooms are hot and the cheese is melted. This dish can be assembled and chilled, covered, 1 day in advance. Bake just before serving.

Serves 6

HINT—The longer you cook garlic, the more delicate its flavor becomes. If you want a subtle taste, use whole garlic cloves or cut them into large pieces and use in recipes in which the ingredients are simmered. For a stronger flavor, pureé, crush, or mince garlic and add just before serving.

Creamed Spinach

1 (10-ounce) package frozen chopped spinach, thawed
2 tablespoons butter or margarine
2 tablespoons flour
1 cup milk
1/4 teaspoon salt
Freshly ground pepper to taste
1 tablespoon grated Parmesan cheese

Drain the spinach, pressing out the excess moisture. Melt the butter in a medium saucepan over medium heat. Stir in the flour to form a paste. Add the milk gradually and cook until thickened, stirring constantly. Add the spinach. Cook over low heat for 5 minutes or until the spinach is tender, stirring constantly. Season with the salt and pepper. Stir in the cheese.

Serves 6

Autumn Squash

9 cups diced peeled Hubbard squash
2 pears, cut into 1-inch pieces
1 cup fresh or thawed frozen cranberries
1 tablespoon margarine
2 tablespoons water

Combine the squash, pears, cranberries, margarine and water in a 3-quart baking dish coated with nonstick cooking spray. Cover and bake at 350 degrees for 50 minutes or until the squash is tender.

Serves 12

Sautéed Tomatoes and Zucchini

2 tablespoons olive oil
1 onion, thinly sliced
2 garlic cloves, minced
1 (15-ounce) can diced tomatoes
2 medium zucchini, thinly sliced
1 yellow or green bell pepper, chopped
2 teaspoons chopped fresh basil, or $1/2$ teaspoon dried basil
$1/8$ to $1/4$ teaspoon pepper
2 tablespoons grated Parmesan cheese

Heat the olive oil in a large skillet over medium heat. Add the onion and garlic. Sauté until the onion is tender. Stir in the undrained tomatoes, zucchini, bell pepper, basil and pepper. Cover and cook for 5 minutes or until the zucchini is tender-crisp, stirring occasionally. Uncover and cook for 5 minutes or until most of the liquid evaporates and the zucchini is tender. Sprinkle with the cheese.

Serves 6

HINT—Vegetables are at their best when their greens, reds, and yellows remain bright. Boiling or sautéing diminishes the colors and reduces much of their nutritional value.

Dilly Zucchini Casserole

1 cup baking mix
1/2 cup (2 ounces) grated Parmesan
  cheese
1 tablespoon chopped fresh dill weed
1 teaspoon salt

1/8 teaspoon pepper
4 eggs, beaten
1/4 cup vegetable oil
3 cups chopped zucchini
1 large onion, chopped

Combine the baking mix, cheese, dill weed, salt and pepper in a large bowl and mix well. Add the eggs and oil and mix well. Stir in the zucchini and onion. Pour into a greased 1 1/2-quart baking dish. Bake at 375 degrees for 25 to 30 minutes or until golden brown.

Serves 5

HINT—Experiment with herbs. Crumble the leaves and discard the stems. Try dill weed in a sauce or sprinkled over cooked vegetables; use both the seeds and leaves.

Marinated Grilled Vegetables

1/2 cup red wine vinegar or cider
  vinegar
1/4 cup olive oil
2 garlic cloves, minced
1/2 teaspoon basil
1/2 teaspoon thyme
1/2 teaspoon lemon pepper

1 pound asparagus
1 large red onion, sliced and separated
  into rings
1 large red bell pepper, cut into
  1-inch strips
1 large yellow bell pepper, cut into
  1-inch strips

Combine the vinegar, olive oil, garlic, basil, thyme and lemon pepper in a large sealable plastic bag and mix well. Add the asparagus, red onion and bell peppers. Seal and turn to coat the vegetables with the marinade. Chill for 1 hour or up to 8 hours, turning once. Drain and reserve the marinade. Place the vegetables in a grill basket or disposable aluminum foil pan with slits cut in the bottom. Place on a grill over hot coals. Grill for 5 minutes. Turn the vegetables, baste with the reserved marinade and grill for 5 to 8 minutes longer or until the vegetables are tender.

Serves 6

Couscous with Artichoke Hearts and Walnuts

1 cup water
1 1/2 cups couscous
3 tablespoons olive oil
1 teaspoon salt
5 artichoke hearts
1/2 cup minced green onions
1 large garlic clove, minced
1 cup chopped fresh parsley

1 to 2 tablespoons fresh dill weed, or
   1 teaspoon dried dill weed
1 tablespoon chopped fresh mint or
   tarragon
Juice of 1/2 lemon
1/2 cup chopped walnuts, toasted
Salt and pepper to taste

Bring the water to a boil in a small saucepan. Combine the boiling water and the couscous in a large heatproof bowl. Stir in the olive oil and salt. Let stand, covered, for 5 minutes. Cut each artichoke heart into 8 pieces. Add the artichoke hearts, green onions, garlic, parsley, dill weed and mint to the couscous and mix well. Stir in the lemon juice, toasted walnuts, salt and pepper.

Serves 4 to 6

Mushroom Pilaf

1 cup (2 sticks) butter
1 cup chopped onion
1 cup chopped celery
8 ounces mushrooms, sliced
2 1/2 cups rice

2 (14-ounce) cans chicken broth
1/2 teaspoon thyme
1/4 teaspoon pepper
1/4 teaspoon salt
1/2 cup chopped fresh parsley

Melt the butter in a large skillet. Add the onion, celery and mushrooms and sauté until the vegetables are tender. Stir in the rice. Bring the chicken broth, thyme, pepper and salt to a boil in a saucepan. Pour the chicken broth mixture into the rice mixture and mix well. Bring to a boil. Reduce the heat and simmer, covered, until the liquid is absorbed. Stir in the parsley.

Serves 6

Fried Rice with Vegetables

5 tablespoons peanut oil

2 eggs, beaten

1 carrot, cut into matchstick-size pieces

2 green onions, chopped

1 cup chopped celery

1/2 cup frozen green peas

3 cups cooked rice

1 tablespoon soy sauce

1/2 teaspoon salt

1/4 teaspoon pepper

Heat the peanut oil in a wok or heavy skillet. Stir the eggs into the oil. Add the carrot, green onions and celery and sauté until tender-crisp. Add the peas, rice and soy sauce and mix well. Cook for 2 minutes. Stir in the salt and pepper. You may substitute other vegetables such as broccoli, zucchini, mushrooms or bell peppers.

Serves 4 to 6

Primavera Risotto

1/4 cup (1/2 stick) butter, divided

1/4 cup chopped onion

1 cup arborio rice

1/4 cup white wine

3 cups vegetable stock

1/4 cup asparagus, blanched and sliced

1/4 cup diced yellow squash or zucchini

1/4 cup julienned red bell pepper

1/4 cup sliced mushrooms

2 tablespoons grated Parmesan cheese

Salt and pepper to taste

Melt 3 tablespoons of the butter in a large skillet. Add the onion and sauté until tender. Add the rice and sauté for 2 minutes. Add the wine and cook until the liquid is absorbed, stirring frequently. Bring the vegetable stock to a simmer in a small saucepan. Add a small amount of the stock at a time to the rice, cooking over low heat after each addition for about 20 minutes or until all of the liquid is absorbed, stirring constantly. Melt the remaining 1 tablespoon butter in a skillet. Add the asparagus, yellow squash, bell pepper and mushrooms and sauté over medium-high heat for 5 minutes or until tender. Stir the vegetables into the rice. Stir in the cheese, salt and pepper.

Serves 2

Glistening Endings

Desserts

South Dakota Winter • *Jayne Erickson Photography*

Winter comes early in South Dakota, often arriving at the end of October. Winter months can be long and cold, but the season is radiant when powdery snow covers the ground and ice glistens on tree branches. The brisk weather does not stop those who love to snow ski, ice skate, snowmobile, and hunt.

We welcome spring's arrival with tulips, crocuses, and daffodils in full bloom. Flocks of geese appear almost daily as they make their way north. Gardeners eagerly prepare their flowerbeds and vegetable gardens while anticipating the vibrant summer colors and fresh produce.

Summer in South Dakota creates a season full of green prairie grasses, brightly colored flowers, and meticulous rows of farm crops. Our days are spent basking by lakes, hiking and horseback riding through the Black Hills, and camping along the Missouri River.

The cool crisp autumnal air arrives in mid-September and lasts until the first snow. Summer blossoms are replaced by brilliant shades of red and gold. South Dakotans enjoy attending fall festivals, picking apples at the orchard, and searching for the best pumpkin in the patch.

Whether you want something flaky, creamy, or decadent, this collection of desserts has as much variety as the seasons of South Dakota. Just as we treasure the beauty of a shimmering blue lake in summer or an icy day in winter, you will appreciate how these desserts bring your meal to a glistening ending.

Chocolate Brownie Crème Brûlée

BROWNIE AND CRÈME BRÛLÉE

3/4 cup (4 1/2 ounces) semisweet chocolate chips

1/4 cup (1/2 stick) unsalted butter

1 cup plus 2 tablespoons sugar, divided

1/2 teaspoon vanilla extract

1/4 teaspoon salt

1 egg

1/2 cup flour

1/2 cup chopped walnuts

5 egg yolks

2 cups heavy cream

1 tablespoon vanilla extract

CHOCOLATE GLAZE

1/2 cup (3 ounces) semisweet chocolate chips

1/4 cup heavy cream

1/2 teaspoon vanilla extract

1 tablespoon light corn syrup

For the brownie, place the chocolate chips and butter in a microwave-safe bowl. Microwave, loosely covered, on High for 1 minute. Stir and microwave for 30-second intervals until the mixture is melted and smooth. Cool for 10 minutes. Whisk in 1/2 cup of the sugar, 1/2 teaspoon vanilla and salt. Whisk in the egg. Stir in the flour just until mixed. Stir in the walnuts. Pour into a greased and floured 8×8-inch baking pan. Bake at 350 degrees for 25 to 30 minutes or until the brownie begins to pull away from the sides of the pan. Let cool completely.

For the crème brûlée, beat the egg yolks and 1/2 cup of the sugar in a mixing bowl until thick. Bring the cream to a simmer in a medium saucepan. Whisk the hot cream into the egg yolk mixture gradually. Whisk in 1 tablespoon vanilla. Pour over the brownie. Place the brownie pan in a larger baking pan. Add water to the larger pan to a depth of 1 inch. Bake at 325 degrees for 45 to 55 minutes or until almost set. Remove from the water bath. Cool, covered, at room temperature. Chill, covered with foil, for 8 hours. Sprinkle the remaining 2 tablespoons sugar evenly over the crème brûlée. Broil for 2 minutes or just until the sugar melts and turns golden brown. Chill for 2 hours.

For the chocolate glaze, combine the chocolate chips, cream, vanilla and corn syrup in a microwave-safe bowl. Microwave, loosely covered, on Low until smooth, stirring occasionally. Spread the chocolate glaze over the the crème brûlée. Chill for 2 hours.

Serves 12

Molten Chocolate Cakes

7¹/2 ounces bittersweet chocolate, coarsely chopped, divided
¹/2 cup plus 3 tablespoons unsalted butter, cut into large pieces
3 eggs
3 egg yolks
¹/4 cup plus 2 tablespoons sugar
5 tablespoons flour, sifted

Place 5¹/2 ounces of the chocolate and the butter in a metal bowl over a pan of simmering water. Heat until melted and smooth, stirring frequently. Remove the bowl and let the chocolate mixture cool slightly. Beat the eggs, egg yolks and sugar at high speed in a mixing bowl for 10 minutes or until pale and thick. Reduce the speed and gradually add the flour, beating constantly. Add the chocolate mixture and beat for 5 minutes or until thick and glossy. Pour half the batter into six 6-ounce buttered and floured custard cups.

Place the remaining 2 ounces chocolate in the center of each cup, using about 1 tablespoon chocolate per cup. Top with the remaining batter. Bake at 325 degrees for 12 minutes or until the cake is set around the edge but the center is not quite set. Remove from the oven and cool for 5 minutes. Run a sharp knife around the edge. Turn the cakes out onto plates. Sprinkle with confectioners' sugar or add a dollop of whipped cream, raspberries or mint sprigs if desired.

Serves 6

HINT—These cakes work very well when made ahead of time, covered with plastic wrap, and chilled until ready to bake. Add 5 to 7 minutes to the baking time for chilled cakes. Semisweet chocolate may be substituted for the bittersweet chocolate if desired.

Chocolate Truffle Cheesecake

CHOCOLATE CRUST

1 1/2 cups chocolate wafer crumbs
2 tablespoons sugar

1/4 cup (1/2 stick) butter or margarine,
   melted

CHEESECAKE

1 3/4 cup (10 1/2 ounces) semisweet
   chocolate chips, divided
1/2 cup heavy cream, divided
24 ounces cream cheese, softened

1 cup sugar
1/3 cup baking cocoa
3 eggs
2 teaspoons vanilla extract, divided

For the crust, combine the cookie crumbs and sugar in a bowl. Stir in the butter. Press onto the bottom and 1 1/2 inches up the side of a greased 9-inch springform pan. Bake at 350 degrees for 10 minutes. Cool on a wire rack. Reduce the oven temperature to 325 degrees.

For the cheesecake, melt 1/4 cup of the chocolate chips in a saucepan over low heat, stirring frequently. Remove from the heat. Stir in 1/4 cup of the cream and mix well. Beat the cream cheese and sugar at high speed in a mixing bowl until light and fluffy. Add the baking cocoa and beat well. Add the eggs and beat at low speed just until blended. Stir in 1 teaspoon of the vanilla and the melted chocolate and beat just until blended. Pour into the crust. Bake at 325 degrees for 45 to 50 minutes or until the center is almost set. Remove from the oven. Let stand until cool.

Melt the remaining 1 1/2 cups chocolate chips in a saucepan over low heat, stirring frequently. Remove from the heat. Stir in the remaining 1/4 cup cream and 1 teaspoon vanilla and mix well. Spread over the cooled cheesecake. Chill, covered, for 8 hours. Loosen the cheesecake from the side of the pan and remove. Garnish with whipped cream and miniature chocolate kisses.

Serves 12

HINT—When whipping heavy cream, there are various ways to ensure success. Pour the cream into a bowl and place it, along with the whisk, in the freezer for 10 minutes just before whipping. To further stabilize the cream, add 2 tablespoons nonfat dry milk powder to every cup of whipping cream before you whip it.

Chocolate Almond Cheesecake

CHOCOLATE ALMOND CRUST

1/2 (1-pound 2-ounce package) chocolate sandwich cookies, crushed
1/4 cup finely chopped almonds
3 tablespoons brown sugar
1/4 cup (1/2 stick) butter, melted

FILLING

24 ounces cream cheese, softened
3 eggs
3 tablespoons milk
1 teaspoon almond extract
3/4 cup packed brown sugar
11/2 cups (9 ounces) chocolate chips

For the crust, combine the cookies, almonds and brown sugar in a bowl. Stir in the melted butter and mix well. Press onto the bottom of a 10-inch springform pan. Bake at 325 degrees for 10 minutes. Remove from the oven and cool.

For the filling, beat the cream cheese in a mixing bowl until light and fluffy. Add the eggs, milk and almond extract and mix well. Add the brown sugar and beat until smooth. Melt the chocolate chips in a double boiler over simmering water. (Or, place the chocolate chips in a microwave-safe bowl and microwave on Low until the chocolate melts, stirring occasionally.) Stir the chocolate into the cream cheese mixture. Pour into the crust. Bake at 325 degrees for 35 to 40 minutes or just until the center is set. Remove from the oven and cool for 20 minutes on a wire rack. Loosen the cheesecake from the side of the pan with a sharp knife. Cool the cheesecake to room temperature. Chill, covered, until the cheesecake is cold. Remove the cheesecake from the pan just before serving.

Serves 12

Mile-High New York-Style Cheesecake

GRAHAM CRACKER CRUST
1½ cups graham cracker crumbs
¼ cup sugar
½ cup (1 stick) butter, softened

FILLING
24 ounces cream cheese, softened
1½ cups sugar
⅛ teaspoon salt
4 eggs, at room temperature
1 teaspoon vanilla extract

TOPPING
2 cups sour cream
¼ cup sugar
1 teaspoon vanilla extract

For the crust, combine the cracker crumbs and sugar in a bowl. Add the butter and mix well. Press onto the bottom and up the side of a 10-inch springform pan. Press heavy-duty foil tightly over the bottom and side of the springform pan to prevent leakage.

For the filling, beat the cream cheese, sugar and salt at medium speed in a mixing bowl for 20 minutes. Add the eggs 1 at a time, mixing well after each addition. Add the vanilla and mix well, scraping the bowl frequently. Pour the filling into the crust. Bake at 350 degrees for 45 to 50 minutes or until the cheesecake is almost set. Remove the cheesecake from the oven. Increase oven temperature to 450 degrees.

For the topping, combine the sour cream, sugar and vanilla in a bowl and mix well. Pour over the cheesecake. Bake at 450 degrees for 10 minutes. Cool completely. Loosen the cheesecake from the side of the pan with a sharp knife. Chill, covered, until ready to serve. Top with fresh fruit.

Serves 16

HINT—Clean-cut slices of cheesecake can be achieved by either heating the knife over an open flame or running it under very warm water before each cut and then cleaning it after each slice is made. Or, try slicing with a long strand of clean dental floss held taut.

Pumpkin Cheesecake with Sour Cream Topping

GRAHAM CRACKER CRUST

1 1/2 cups graham cracker crumbs

1/4 cup sugar

1/3 cup butter or margarine, melted

FILLING

24 ounces cream cheese, softened

1 cup packed brown sugar

1 (16-ounce) can pumpkin

2 tablespoons cornstarch

1 1/4 teaspoons cinnamon

1/2 teaspoon nutmeg

1 (5-ounce) can evaporated milk

2 eggs

TOPPING

2 cups sour cream

1/3 cup sugar

1 teaspoon vanilla extract

For the crust, combine the cracker crumbs and sugar in a bowl. Add the butter and mix well. Press onto the bottom and 1 1/2 inches up the side of a 9-inch springform pan. Bake at 350 degrees for 5 to 7 minutes or until set. Cool for 10 minutes.

For the filling, beat the cream cheese and brown sugar in a mixing bowl until light and fluffy. Add the pumpkin, cornstarch, cinnamon and nutmeg and mix well. Gradually beat in the evaporated milk and eggs just until blended. Pour into the crust. Bake at 350 degrees for 55 to 60 minutes or until the center is almost set.

For the topping, stir the sour cream, sugar and vanilla together in a bowl. Spread over the filling. Bake at 350 degrees for 5 minutes. Cool on a wire rack for 10 minutes. Loosen the cheesecake from the side of the pan with a sharp knife. Cool the cheesecake for 1 hour. Chill, covered, for 8 hours. Remove the cheesecake from the pan and let stand for 30 minutes before slicing. Sprinkle with cinnamon if desired.

Serves 12 to 14

Kuchen (Hunklich)

CRUST

1/2 cup (1 stick) butter, softened
1/4 cup sugar
2 eggs
1/2 teaspoon salt

1 cup lukewarm milk
1 tablespoon yeast mixed with
    1/2 cup flour
4 cups (about) flour

PASTRY CREAM

1 3/4 cups milk
1/3 cup semolina (high gluten
    flour)
1/2 cup plus 2 tablespoons
    sugar, divided
Pinch of salt
3 egg whites

4 cups drained canned sour cherries,
    sliced peaches or mandarin oranges
    or 4 cups fresh berries or sliced
    plums in season
2 cups sour cream
3 egg yolks
1 tablespoon melted butter

For the crust, cream the butter and sugar in a mixing bowl until light and fluffy. Add the eggs 1 at a time, mixing well after each addition. Add the salt. Stir in the milk, yeast mixture and flour, adding additional flour if necessary to make a soft dough. Place in a greased bowl, turning to coat the surface. Let rise, covered, in a warm place until doubled in bulk. Punch the dough down. Roll into an 11×17-inch rectangle on a lightly floured surface. Place in a greased 11×17-inch baking pan, pressing the dough up the side of the pan.

For the pastry cream, bring the milk to a boil in a saucepan over high heat. Add the semolina. Cook over medium heat until the mixture thickens, stirring constantly. Add 2 tablespoons of the sugar and the salt and mix well. Cook for 5 minutes. Let stand until cool. Beat the egg whites at high speed in a mixing bowl until stiff peaks form. Fold the egg whites into the semolina mixture. Spread the mixture over the crust. Top with the fruit. Combine the sour cream, remaining 1/2 cup sugar, egg yolks and butter in a bowl and mix well. Spread over the fruit. Bake at 375 degrees for 20 minutes or until light brown and set. Serve warm or at room temperature.

Serves 18 to 24

HINT—Kuchen simply means "cake" in German. Brought to our state by our German immigrant ancestors, this traditional dessert is generally considered a yeast-raised coffee cake topped with pastry cream and fruit. This particular cake recipe is called Hunklich, or "Saxon Pie," and comes to us from Transylvanian Saxons. Kuchen was adopted as the state dessert of South Dakota in 2000.

Strawberry Tart

NUT CRUST
1¼ cups finely chopped walnuts or almonds
½ cup (1 stick) unsalted butter, softened
3½ tablespoons plus 1 teaspoon sugar
1½ cups flour
1 egg, beaten
½ teaspoon vanilla or almond extract

FILLING
Whole strawberries, hulled (about 3 pints)

RED CURRANT GLAZE
1 (6-ounce) jar red currant jelly
1 tablespoon plain gelatin
¼ cup Grand Marnier or Cognac

ASSEMBLY
1 cup whipping cream, whipped

For the crust, combine the walnuts, butter, sugar, flour, egg and vanilla in a mixing bowl and mix to form a dough. Pat the dough into a buttered 9-inch tart pan with a removable bottom or twelve 3-inch tartlet pans. Chill, covered, for 30 minutes. Bake at 350 degrees for 15 to 20 minutes or until golden brown. Cool the crust to room temperature.

For the filling, arrange the strawberries hull side down on the crust.

For the glaze, heat the jelly in a saucepan. Dissolve the gelatin in the Grand Marnier in a small bowl and add to the jelly. Cook over low heat until the mixture is clear, stirring constantly. Spoon or brush the glaze over the berries. Serve with the whipped cream.

Serves 6 to 8

HINT—You may substitute 2½ cups fresh red currants, 1 quart blueberries or halved seedless grapes, or thinly sliced kiwifruit for the strawberries. Use strained apricot jam in place of the red currant jelly.

Mascarpone Fruit Tart

CRUST

1 refrigerator pie pastry
1 to 2 teaspoons milk

2 tablespoons sugar

FILLING

8 ounces mascarpone cheese,
   softened
2/3 cup heavy cream

1/3 cup sugar
2 teaspoons vanilla extract

TOPPING

3 tablespoons apricot preserves
1 tablespoon water
1 pint (heaping) strawberries, halved

1 cup raspberries
1 cup blueberries

For the crust, unfold the pastry into a 9- or 10-inch tart pan or pie plate. Remove the plastic wrap. Fit the pastry into the pan and trim the edge. Brush with the milk and sprinkle with the sugar. Prick the pastry with a fork. Bake at 450 degrees for 8 to 12 minutes or until golden brown. Remove from the oven and cool completely.

For the filling, beat the cheese, cream, sugar and vanilla at high speed in a mixing bowl just until stiff peaks form. Spread over the pie crust.

For the topping, combine the apricot preserves and water in a large microwave-safe bowl. Microwave on Medium until the preserves melt. Gently stir in the strawberries, raspberries and blueberries. Spoon the berries over the filling. Chill, covered, until ready to serve.

Serves 8 to 12

HINT—Mascarpone cheese is similar in texture to cream cheese. It comes from Italy and Switzerland and is probably best known for its use in tiramisu. Made from cow's milk, mascarpone has a mild flavor and pairs wonderfully with fresh fruit.

Raspberry and Peach Cobbler

2^1/$_2$ pounds peaches, peeled and sliced
2 cups raspberries
1^1/$_4$ cups sugar, divided
2 tablespoons water
^{1}/$_4$ teaspoon almond extract
1 cup flour
^{1}/$_2$ cup (1 stick) unsalted butter
1 cup whipping cream, whipped, or vanilla ice cream

Arrange the peach slices in a 9×13-inch baking dish. Top with the raspberries. Combine ^{3}/$_4$ cup of the sugar, the water and almond extract in a small bowl and mix well. Pour over the fruit. Combine the flour and remaining ^{1}/$_2$ cup sugar in a medium bowl. Cut in the butter until crumbly. Sprinkle the flour mixture evenly over the fruit. Bake at 350 degrees for 50 minutes. Cool to room temperature. Serve with the whipped cream.

Serves 8 to 10

HINT—You may use pears or other seasonal berries in this versatile dessert. Strawberry-blueberry or strawberry-rhubarb combinations are wonderful. Simply use 2 cups of each fruit for the substitution. When using rhubarb, you may want to add an additional ^{1}/$_3$ cup sugar as rhubarb is quite tart.

Frozen Berry Dessert

VANILLA WAFER CRUST
1¹/2 cups crushed vanilla wafers, divided
1/2 cup (1 stick) butter or margarine, melted

FILLING
1 cup sugar
1 (10-ounce) package frozen mixed berries, partially thawed
2 egg whites
1/4 teaspoon salt
2 tablespoons lemon juice
1 cup whipped topping

For the crust, combine 1 cup plus 6 tablespoons of the wafer crumbs and the butter in a bowl and mix well. Press into a 9×13-inch baking pan.

For the filling, beat the sugar, berries, egg whites, salt and lemon juice at high speed in a mixing bowl for 20 minutes. Fold in the whipped topping. Pour into the crust. Sprinkle with the remaining 2 tablespoons wafer crumbs. Freeze, covered, for 6 to 8 hours.

Serves 18

HINT—As a substitute for raw eggs, use meringue powder and follow the package directions.

Holiday Ice Cream Dessert

1/2 gallon vanilla ice cream
3/4 cup raspberry liqueur
1 pint raspberries
2 or 3 kiwifruit, sliced

Place 1 scoop of ice cream in each of 6 dessert dishes. Pour 1 to 2 tablespoons liqueur over the ice cream. Top with the raspberries and kiwifruit.

Serves 6

Peanut Butter and Chocolate Mousse Torte

PEANUT BUTTER MOUSSE

2 cups confectioners' sugar, divided

3/4 cup plus 2 tablespoons creamy
    peanut butter

6 ounces cream cheese, softened

3 tablespoons heavy cream

2 egg whites

CHOCOLATE MOUSSE

8 ounces chocolate chips

1 1/2 teaspoons instant coffee

2 1/2 tablespoons hot water

3 egg yolks

1 cup whipping cream

1/3 cup sugar

CHOCOLATE GLAZE

2/3 cup heavy cream

5 tablespoons unsalted butter

5 ounces chocolate chips

For the peanut butter mousse, combine 1 1/3 cups of the confectioners' sugar, the peanut butter and cream cheese in a large mixing bowl and beat until blended. Add the cream and mix well. Beat the egg whites in a mixing bowl until soft peaks form. Add the remaining 2/3 cup confectioners' sugar gradually and beat until stiff peaks form. Fold the egg white mixture into the peanut butter mixture 1/2 at a time. Line a 6-cup loaf pan with foil. Tilt the prepared pan to a 45-degree angle. Spoon the peanut butter mixture into the pan and smooth the top. (The mousse will form a triangle along the length of the pan.) Freeze, covered, for 1 hour or until firm, propping to maintain the 45-degree angle.

For the chocolate mousse, microwave the chocolate chips in a microwave-safe bowl until melted. Let stand for 5 minutes. Dissolve the instant coffee in the hot water in a small bowl. Whisk in the egg yolks. Add the egg yolk mixture to the melted chocolate, stirring until the mixture is smooth and slightly thickened. Let stand until cooled to room temperature. Combine the whipping cream and sugar in a mixing bowl and beat until soft peaks form. Fold the whipped cream into the chocolate mixture 1/2 at a time. Spoon the chocolate mixture over the frozen peanut butter mousse in the upright pan and smooth the top. Freeze, covered, for 6 to 8 hours or until firm.

For the glaze, combine the cream, butter and chocolate chips in a microwave-safe bowl. Microwave on Low until blended, stirring occasionally. Chill, covered, for 4 to 8 hours.

To assemble, invert the frozen torte onto a cake rack, removing the foil. Spread the glaze over the mousse. Place on a serving platter. Freeze, covered, for 1 to 2 hours or until the glaze is set. Slice and serve with sweetened whipped cream or cream flavored with caramel sauce.

Serves 12 to 16

Apple Cake with Caramel Sauce

CAKE

2 eggs

4 cups finely chopped peeled apples

2 cups sugar

2 teaspoons cinnamon

1/2 cup vegetable oil

2 cups flour

2 teaspoons baking soda

1 teaspoon salt

CARAMEL SAUCE

1/2 cup (1 stick) butter

1/2 cup sugar

1/2 cup packed brown sugar

1/2 teaspoon vanilla extract

1/2 cup half-and-half

For the cake, beat the eggs in a large mixing bowl. Add the apples and mix well. Stir in the sugar. Add the cinnamon, oil, flour, baking soda and salt and mix well. The batter will be thick. Pour into a greased 9×13-inch cake pan. Bake at 350 degrees for 45 minutes.

For the sauce, melt the butter in a saucepan. Stir in the sugar, brown sugar, vanilla and half-and-half. Bring to a boil to dissolve the sugar, stirring occasionally. Serve warm over the cake.

Serves 12 to 16

Pineapple Cake

CAKE

2 eggs, beaten

2 cups sugar

2 cups flour

2 teaspoons baking soda

1 (20-ounce) can crushed pineapple

1 teaspoon vanilla extract

1/2 cup chopped walnuts

CREAM CHEESE AND WALNUT FROSTING

1/4 cup (1/2 stick) margarine, softened

8 ounces cream cheese, softened

1 1/3 cups confectioners' sugar

1/2 cup crushed walnuts

1 teaspoon vanilla extract

For the cake, combine the ingredients in the order listed in a mixing bowl and mix well. Pour into a 9×13-inch cake pan. Bake at 350 degrees for 45 minutes.

For the frosting, cream the margarine, cream cheese and confectioners' sugar in a mixing bowl until light and fluffy. Stir in the walnuts and vanilla. Spread over the warm cake.

Serves 18

Chocolate Raspberry Cake

1 cup plus 2 tablespoons unsalted butter
2 tablespoons framboise (raspberry brandy)
10 ounces bittersweet chocolate or semisweet chocolate, coarsely chopped
1/2 cup sugar
1/2 cup packed brown sugar
1 1/2 cups coffee, or 1 tablespoon instant coffee dissolved in 1 1/2 cups water
1 1/3 cups self-rising flour
1/4 cup baking cocoa
2 eggs
1 pint raspberries
Confectioners' sugar

Line a 10-inch springform pan or 10-inch cake pan with parchment paper or waxed paper. Spray with cooking spray. Wrap foil around the outside bottom of the pan.

Combine the butter, framboise, chocolate, sugar, brown sugar and coffee in a large saucepan. Cook over low heat until the butter and chocolate are melted, stirring occasionally. Remove from the heat. Add the flour and baking cocoa and whisk until smooth. Beat in the eggs. The batter will be thin. Sprinkle the raspberries in the prepared pan. Pour the batter over the raspberries. Bake at 350 degrees for 45 minutes. Cool for 20 minutes. Remove from the pan. Dust with confectioners' sugar. Serve warm or at room temperature.

Serves 16

No-Bake Cheesecake Pie

1 cup (6 ounces) white chocolate chips
16 ounces cream cheese, cut into small chunks
8 ounces frozen whipped topping, thawed
1 (9-inch) graham cracker pie shell
1/3 cup English toffee bits or almond brickle chips

Melt the white chocolate chips in a heavy saucepan over medium-low heat, stirring constantly. Remove from the heat. Blend in the cream cheese. Fold in the whipped topping. Pour into the crust. Chill, covered, for 8 hours or until set. Sprinkle with the toffee bits.

Serves 6 to 8

Frozen Chocolate Gelato Pie

CHOCOLATE COOKIE CRUST

3/4 cup chocolate sandwich cookie crumbs

3 tablespoons butter, melted

FILLING

1 1/4 cups plus 1/3 cup miniature marshmallows, divided

1 cup (6 ounces) milk chocolate chips

1/2 cup (3 ounces) semisweet chocolate chips

1/2 cup light cream or half-and-half

1 cup heavy cream

2/3 cup roasted salted almonds, coarsely chopped

TOPPING

1/2 cup heavy cream

5 tablespoons unsalted butter

5 ounces semisweet chocolate

For the crust, combine the cookie crumbs and butter in a bowl and mix well. Press onto the bottom and side of a 9-inch deep-dish pie plate. Bake at 300 degrees for 10 minutes. Let stand until cool.

For the filling, combine 1 1/4 cups of the marshmallows, the milk chocolate chips, semisweet chocolate chips and light cream in a microwave-safe bowl. Microwave on High until melted and smooth, stirring frequently. Let cool completely. Beat the heavy cream in a small chilled mixing bowl just until it holds a shape. Fold the whipped cream into the chocolate mixture 1/4 at a time. Stir in the chopped almonds and remaining 1/3 cup miniature marshmallows. Spoon the filling into the crust and smooth the top. Freeze, covered, for 2 hours.

For the topping, combine the cream, butter and chocolate in a microwave-safe bowl. Microwave on High until smooth, stirring frequently. Cool to room temperature. Pour over the filling. Freeze, covered, for 2 hours.

Serves 8 to 12

Chocolate Peanut Butter Pie

CRUST

1 cup graham cracker crumbs

1/4 cup (1/2 stick) butter, melted

2 tablespoons sugar

FILLING

1 1/4 cups (7 1/2 ounces) semisweet
   chocolate chips

2 2/3 cups heavy cream, divided

2 tablespoons light corn syrup

2 teaspoons vanilla extract

1 cup (6 ounces) peanut butter chips

2 tablespoons creamy peanut butter

2 tablespoons sugar

TOPPING

1 cup heavy cream

1/4 cup confectioners' sugar

2 teaspoons vanilla extract

For the crust, combine the cracker crumbs, butter and sugar in a medium bowl and mix well. Press onto the bottom and side of a lightly buttered 9- or 10-inch pie plate. Bake at 350 degrees for 12 to 15 minutes or until light brown. Cool completely.

For the filling, combine the chocolate chips, 2/3 cup of the cream, corn syrup and vanilla in a microwave-safe bowl. Microwave on High for 1 minute. Microwave on Defrost for 3 minutes or until smooth, stirring occasionally. Spread over the cooled crust. Chill, covered, until the chocolate is firm.

Combine 1/2 cup of the cream and the peanut butter chips in a microwave-safe bowl. Microwave on Low until melted, stirring every 30 seconds. Add the peanut butter and stir until smooth. Cool to room temperature. Beat the remaining 1 1/2 cups cream and the sugar in a chilled mixing bowl just until soft peaks begin to form. Do not overbeat. Fold 1 cup of the cream into the peanut butter mixture. Fold in the remaining cream. Spread the peanut butter mixture over the chocolate layer. Chill, covered, for 2 hours or longer.

For the topping, combine the cream, confectioners' sugar and vanilla in a mixing bowl. Beat until stiff peaks form. Spread the topping over the peanut butter layer. Chill, covered, until ready to serve. Decorate with chopped peanuts or chocolate curls if desired.

Serves 6 to 8

Chocolate Chip Cookie Pie

2 eggs
1/2 cup flour
1/2 cup sugar
1/2 cup packed brown sugar

1 cup (2 sticks) butter, melted and cooled
1 cup (6 ounces) semisweet chocolate
    chips
1 unbaked (8-inch) pie shell

Beat the eggs in a bowl. Add the flour, sugar, brown sugar and butter and mix well by hand. Stir in the chocolate chips. Spoon into the pie shell. Bake at 325 degrees for 1 hour.

Serves 6

Pecan Squares

CRUST
3 cups flour
1/2 cup sugar
1/2 teaspoon salt

1 cup (2 sticks) butter or margarine,
    softened

FILLING
4 eggs
1 1/2 cups light or dark corn syrup
1 1/2 cups sugar

3 tablespoons melted butter or margarine
1 1/2 teaspoons vanilla extract
2 1/2 cups chopped pecans

For the crust, combine the flour, sugar and salt in a large bowl. Cut in the butter until crumbly. Press into a greased 10×15-inch baking dish. Bake at 350 degrees for 20 minutes.

For the filling, combine the eggs, corn syrup, sugar, melted butter and vanilla in a large bowl and mix well. Stir in the pecans. Pour the mixture over the hot crust. Bake at 350 degrees for 25 minutes or until set. Cool on a wire rack. Cut into squares.

Makes 4 dozen

GLISTENING ENDINGS

Rhubarb Custard Bars

CRUST
2 cups flour
1/4 cup sugar
1 cup (2 sticks) cold butter or margarine

FILLING
2 cups sugar
7 tablespoons flour
1 cup heavy cream
3 eggs, beaten
5 cups finely chopped rhubarb

TOPPING
6 ounces cream cheese, softened
1/2 cup sugar
1/2 teaspoon vanilla extract
1 cup whipping cream

For the crust, combine the flour and sugar in a bowl. Cut in the butter until crumbly. Press into a greased 9×13-inch baking pan. Bake at 350 degrees for 10 minutes.

For the filling, combine the sugar and flour in a bowl. Whisk in the cream and eggs. Stir in the rhubarb. Pour over the crust. Bake at 350 degrees for 40 to 45 minutes or until the custard is set. Let stand until cool.

For the topping, combine the cream cheese, sugar and vanilla in a mixing bowl and beat until smooth. Whip the cream until soft peaks form. Fold the whipped cream into the cream cheese mixture. Spread over the filling. Chill, covered, until set. Cut into bars to serve.

Makes 3 dozen

Chocolate Butterfinger Cookies

1 1/2 cups sugar
1 1/3 cups packed light or dark brown
   sugar
1/2 cup (1 stick) butter, softened
4 eggs
4 teaspoons vanilla extract
2 1/2 cups chunky peanut butter

2 cups flour
1 teaspoon baking soda
1/2 teaspoon salt
1 (22-ounce) package Butterfinger BB's
   candy
1 cup (6 ounces) milk chocolate chips

    Cream the sugar, brown sugar and butter in a mixing bowl until light and fluffy. Add the eggs and vanilla and mix well. Stir in the peanut butter and mix well. Combine the flour, baking soda and salt in a bowl. Add to the peanut butter mixture and mix well. Stir in the Butterfinger BB's and chocolate chips. Drop by tablespoonfuls onto a foil-lined cookie sheet. Bake at 350 degrees for 8 to 10 minutes or until the cookies are firm and light brown. Cool on the cookie sheet for 5 minutes. Remove to a wire rack to cool completely.

    Makes 4 to 5 dozen

Oatmeal Carmelitas

2 cups plus 4 teaspoons flour, divided
2 cups quick-cooking oats
1 1/2 cups packed brown sugar
1 teaspoon baking soda
1/2 teaspoon salt

1 1/2 cups (3 sticks) butter, melted
1 cup (6 ounces) semisweet chocolate
   chips
1 cup walnut halves
1 (12-ounce) jar caramel topping

    Combine 2 cups flour, the oats, brown sugar, baking soda, salt and melted butter in a large bowl and mix well. Pat 2/3 of the oat mixture in a 9×13-inch baking pan. Bake at 350 degrees for 10 minutes. Sprinkle with the chocolate chips and walnuts. Combine the caramel topping and remaining 4 teaspoons flour in a bowl and mix well. Drizzle over the chocolate chips and walnuts. Sprinkle the remaining 1/3 of the oat mixture on top. Bake at 350 degrees for 15 to 20 minutes or until set. Do not overbake. Cool and cut into bars.

    Makes 2 1/2 dozen

Swedish Cinnamon Cookies

1 cup (2 sticks) butter, softened
1 cup sugar
1 tablespoon molasses
1 teaspoon baking soda

1 egg yolk, beaten
2 cups flour
1 tablespoon cinnamon
Sugar

Cream the butter and sugar in a mixing bowl until light and fluffy. Add the molasses and mix well. Dissolve the baking soda in the egg yolk in a small bowl. Stir into the creamed mixture. Add the flour and cinnamon and mix well. Do not overbeat. Roll the dough into small balls. Roll in additional sugar to coat. Arrange on a nonstick cookie sheet. Bake at 350 degrees for 12 to 14 minutes or until the cookies are slightly firm.

Makes 3 dozen

Lemon and White Chocolate Shortbread

1 cup (2 sticks) butter, softened
1/2 cup confectioners' sugar
1 teaspoon vanilla extract
2 1/4 cups flour

1/4 teaspoon salt
1 (10-ounce) jar lemon curd
2 ounces white chocolate

Cream the butter, confectioners' sugar and vanilla in a mixing bowl until light and fluffy. Add the flour and salt and mix well. Shape the dough into a 4×8-inch rectangle on a large sheet of waxed paper or plastic wrap. Cut into two 2×8-inch rectangles. Cut each rectangle into 1/4-inch slices. Place 1 inch apart on a foil-lined cookie sheet. Bake at 400 degrees for 6 to 9 minutes or until set but not brown. Cool on the cookie sheet for 5 minutes. Remove to a wire rack to cool completely. Spoon the lemon curd into a sealable heavy-duty plastic bag. Snip off 1 corner of the bag. Squeeze a small amount of lemon curd onto each cookie. Place the white chocolate in a sealable heavy-duty plastic bag. Microwave on Medium until the white chocolate melts. Snip off 1 corner of the bag. Drizzle the white chocolate over the lemon curd. Cool on a wire rack until the chocolate sets.

Makes 4 to 6 dozen

HINT—Instead of lemon curd, try other curd flavors such as raspberry, blackberry, or orange. Apricot or raspberry preserves can also be used in place of the lemon curd.

Pillow Cookies

COOKIES

1/2 cup (1 stick) butter, softened
1 cup sugar
1 teaspoon vanilla extract
1 egg

1/2 teaspoon baking powder
2 1/2 cups flour
1/2 cup buttermilk

ALMOND FROSTING

3 tablespoons butter, softened
3 to 3 1/2 cups confectioners' sugar
1/4 cup milk

1 to 2 teaspoons almond extract
Food coloring (optional)

For the cookies, cream the butter, sugar, vanilla and egg in a mixing bowl until light and fluffy. Add the baking powder. Add the flour alternately with the buttermilk, mixing well after each addition. Drop the batter by teaspoonfuls onto a greased cookie sheet. Bake at 375 degrees for 10 to 12 minutes or until the cookies are set and light brown. Cool on the cookie sheet for 5 minutes. Remove to a wire rack to cool completely.

For the frosting, combine the butter, 3 cups confectioners' sugar, milk, almond extract and food coloring in a mixing bowl. Beat until light, adding more confectioners' sugar if necessary. Frost the cookies.

Makes about 4 dozen

Pecan Goodies

2 cups pecan halves
1/4 cup (1/2 stick) butter
1 egg white

1/2 cup sugar
1 teaspoon cinnamon
1/8 teaspoon nutmeg

Place the pecans in an 11×14-inch baking pan. Bake at 325 degrees for 10 minutes. Remove the pecans from the pan. Melt the butter in the pan. Add the pecans and stir to coat with the butter. Beat the egg white in a mixing bowl until foamy. Stir in the sugar, cinnamon and nutmeg. Pour over the pecans. Bake at 325 degrees for 30 minutes, stirring every 10 minutes. Let stand until cool.

Makes 2 1/2 cups

Double Chocolate Truffles

8 ounces semisweet chocolate, melted
1/4 cup amaretto
2 tablespoons strong brewed coffee
1/2 cup (1 stick) unsalted butter, softened
1 tablespoon vanilla extract
3/4 cup vanilla wafer crumbs
14 ounces milk chocolate, melted
1 ounce white chocolate, melted

Combine the semisweet chocolate, amaretto and coffee in a small bowl and mix well. Add the butter, vanilla and wafer crumbs and mix well. Chill, covered, until the mixture is firm, stirring frequently. Form the chocolate mixture into balls. Place on a foil-lined pan. Freeze for 1 hour or until firm. Place the melted milk chocolate in a shallow bowl. Spear the truffles with a wooden pick and dip in the milk chocolate. Place on a waxed paper-lined 11×14-inch pan. Freeze for 10 minutes or until the chocolate is firm. Drizzle with the melted white chocolate. Chill, covered, in the refrigerator. Let the truffles stand at room temperature for a few minutes before serving.

Makes 2 to 3 dozen

HINT—Chilled truffles can be rolled in a mixture of 1/2 cup confectioners' sugar and 1/2 cup baking cocoa instead of the melted chocolate. Substitute orange, raspberry, coffee, or mint-flavored liqueur for the amaretto to create different flavored truffles. Omit the alcohol from the recipe by using an additional 1/4 cup coffee.

Acknowledgments

Dining Dakota Style represents the dedication we feel about the Junior League of Sioux Falls and the pride we feel about our community and state. This endeavor has been possible because of the generous financial contributions as well as the devotion of time, energy, and expertise of several businesses, family, and friends. We express our gratitude to all those listed. It is our hope that no one has been inadvertently overlooked from our list.

CORPORATE SPONSORS

COOKBOOK PARTNERS

Avera McKennan Hospital

The Everist Company

Sioux Valley Hospital

Wells Fargo Bank

Wells Fargo Education Financial Services

Wells Fargo Financial Bank

CHAPTER PARTNERS

First National Bank

Heart Hospital of South Dakota

Home Federal Bank

Howalt-McDowell Insurance Incorporated

Mahlander's Appliance and Lighting

CORPORATE PARTNERS

Lewis Drug Stores

Bell Incorporated

PROMOTIONAL PARTNERS

HenkinSchultz Communication Arts

KSFY Television

Midcontinent Communications

Midcontinent Radio (KELO-FM)

Acknowledgments

MONETARY DONATIONS

Denise* and Richard Abild

Allison* and Greg Alvine

Nadine Amundson*

Melissa* and Brad Anderson

Jean Anstine*

Tamara Baker*

Nicole Barnes

Holly Brunick*

Barbara Everist*

Sandy Farner*

Susan Flynn*

Tansy* and Jason Forbes

Cheryl Gaeckle*

Gretchen Graves*

Lisa Griffin*

Angi Gulbranson*

Susan Hagen*

Bunny Howes*

Julie Jacobsen*

Jeanne Johnson*

Jane Nutter Johnson*

Arlene Kirby*

Peggy Kirby*

Sandy* and Todd Kost

Cathy* and Chris Krueger

Amy* and Jacob Kusmak

Ann* and Bob Lange

Jennifer* and Eric Larson

Collette* and Dr. Dean Madison

Carol McGinnis*

Chris McGrann*

Pam Nelson*

Carol Oakland*

Nancy* and Joe Olsen

Amy* and Mike Olson

Deborah Olson*

Ruth Parry*

Shelley Pate*

Karen Pekas*

Renae* and John Pekas

Lynda* and David Pfeifle

Cynthia Phillips*

Cathy Piersol**

Michele Prestbo*

Shelly* and Dan Rausch

Susan Sabers

Dana Sandene

Liz Sea*

Kim Steinke*

Barb Stork*

Nancee* and Tim Sturdevant

Kris Swanson*

Suzanne Toll*

Kathy and Ray Trankle

Shannon VanBuskirk*

Marilyn VanDemark*

Suzanne* and Jon Veenis

Kathleen Walsh*

Mary and Rick** Weber

Anne West*

Tammy Wyche

IN-KIND DONATIONS

Avera McKennan Fitness Center

BCBG Max Azria

Brandon Golf Course

Buffalo Creek Ranch

CJ Callaway's Kitchen and Restaurant

Century Theatres

Cherry Creek Grill

Citibank of South Dakota

Classic Chef Gourmet Market

Cooking For You

Ducks Unlimited

Ethan Allen Home Interiors

Gary's Gun Shop

Greg Latza, Peoplescapes Publishing

Image Nation

Inn on Westport

JJ's Wine, Spirits and Cigars

Jayne Erickson Photography

Johnny Sundby, Dakota Skies Photography

Josephine's Unique Floral Designery

Kitchen Cordial

Larsen Designs Limited

Mark Kayser Enterprises

Pier One Imports

Rick Albrecht, Massage Therapist

Salon Britori

Scheels All Sports

Sioux Falls Area Chamber of Commerce

Sioux Falls Brewing Company

Sodak Distributing Company

South Dakota Department of Tourism

Spezia's Restaurant

The Diamond Room

The Outfitter

Tom Luke Skin and Body Care

Treasured Gems

Tularosa Groves Pistachios

Two Charming

Zandbroz Variety

Contributors

RECIPE CONTRIBUTORS, TESTERS, AND COOKS

Denise Haerter Abild*	Arli Christenson	Allen Funk	Jackie Hove
Julie Bergan Abraham	KrisAnne Christenson*	Nancy Gjoraas*	Bunny Howes*
Kyle Adams	Paul Cink	Travis Gjoraas	Lynn Hyvonen
Nadine Amundson*	Shirley Cink*	Melanie Glasrud	Julie Jacobsen*
Ruth Amundson	Jen Cisar*	Judy Godbey	Lisa Jervik
Brad Anderson	Chris Clayton	Dan Goeman	Carol Johnson
Melissa Anderson*	Lisa Davis*	Shelli Goeman*	Dave Johnson
Kay Andrus	Kay DeBates	Roberta Goodhope	David Johnson
Mil Andrus	Bobi DeKleinhans	Janet Graff*	Elsa Johnson
Phyllis Bakken	Jim DeKleinhans	Pat Graham*	Jeanne Johnson*
Nicole Barnes	Norma Denison	Gretchen Graves*	Jane Nutter Johnson*
Brent Bartels	Laurie Dolan	Beth Green	Kim Johnson*
Emily Bartels*	Joan Donahoe*	Kyle Greenfield*	Mike Johnson
Jane Laase Becker	Dan Donohue	Lisa Griffin*	Heidi Kickul
Jan Bergan	Dorothy Donahue*	Kris Gross	Arlene Kirby*
Chris Bills	Laura Donahue	Angi Gulbranson*	Jennifer Kirby
Shawn Bills	Becky Dunlap	Bethany Gusso	Lisa Kiroff
Dar Blanchard*	Dave Edwards	Dawn Gutnik*	Cathy Kjorness
Beth Boyens	Jennifer Edwards*	Susan Hagen*	Anita Klune
Lori Brekke	Carolyn Eisenbeisz	Danylle Hampton*	Judy Knudson
Kris Brende	Leslie Elliott*	Deb Harkema	Amy Knuth
Lotta Breyer	Monica Fehrs*	Linda Hartmann*	Donna Knutson
Margaret Donohue Bruggeman*	Dee Fletcher	Beverly Harvey*	Russ Knutson
Christine Burg*	Mike Flynn	Susan Hedge*	Susan Kolb
Adrienne Burla	Sue Flynn*	Cathy Hennies	Bill Koons
Jody Weeg Carstens	Beth Fodness	Beth Henry	Sandy Kost*
Mike Childers	Sally Fodness	Kathy Hines	Cheryl Krier
Moria Nelson Childers	Jason Forbes	Mike Hines	Tracy Kroon*
Tanisha Nelson Childers	Tansy Forbes*	Arlene Horner	Cathy Krueger*

Contributors

RECIPE CONTRIBUTORS, TESTERS, AND COOKS

Chris Krueger	Sonja Niles	Sue Salem	Jon Veenis
Vasanth Kuchangi	Charlotte Noonan	Dana Sandene	Suzanne Veenis*
Jody Kusek*	Penny Nordstrom*	Jamie Schaefer*	Garett Voecks
Amy Trankle Kusmak*	Julie Norton	Liz Sea*	Shelly Voecks*
Carmen Kusmak	Joe Olsen	Susan Segelon	Paula Vreeland
Jacob Kusmak	Nancy Olsen*	Christy Sequoia	Kathy Walsh*
Matty Kusmak	Tom Olsen**	Sarah Sharp*	Carol Ward
Ann Lange	Amy Olson*	Denise Shields	Jerry Ward
Deb Larson	Mike Olson	Terri Smith	Amy Warren
Eric Larson	Cheryl Paetow	Donna Smithback	Kim Wassink*
Jennifer Larson*	Shelley Pate*	Michelle Sodorff	Rick Weber**
Joan Larson	Steve Pate	Roxy Soll	Ann Weeg
John Larson	John Pekas	Matt Sorrell	Coryill Weeg
Tom Larson	Renae Pekas*	Kim Steinke*	Kelly Wiebenga
Kim Lawrenz*	Tara Petersen	Dawn Stenberg*	Paul Wyche
Heidi Leist	Juli Peterson	Linnea Strande	Tammy Wyche
Lorrae Lindquist*	Kristen Peterson*	Nancee Sturdevant*	Jayne Zielenski
Heather Loehrer	Sue Peterson	Tim Sturdevant	
Kristin Loehrer	Dave Pfeifle	Kris Swanson*	
Kathy Luke*	Lynda Pfeifle*	Carla Swift	*Denotes a member
Melissa Maldonado*	Anita Phelps	Helga Szameit	of the Junior League
Carol McGinnis*	Cyndi Phillips*	Jeni Bergan Thomas*	of Sioux Falls
Gail Meader*	Lori Potratz	Barbara Tinsdale	
Julie Meyer	Shelly Rausch*	Larry Toll	
Linda Mofle*	Margaret Reardon	Suzanne Toll*	**Denotes a community
Patricia Naughton	DeAnn Reker	Betty Trankle	advisory board
Donna Nelsen	Kay Rozell	Kathy Trankle	member of the
Pam Nelson*	Sharon Rueschhoff	Shannon VanBuskirk*	Junior League of
Penny Newbauer	Susan Sabers	Cheryl VanNoort	Sioux Falls

Professional Photography Credits

The Junior League of Sioux Falls would like to thank the photographers who generously
gave their gift of time and talent to capture the beauty of our city and state.

JAYNE ERICKSON

Jayne Erickson, an award winning freelance photographer for over twenty years, has received two prestigious Kodak Gallery Awards, the Fuji Masterpiece Award for outstanding illustration photography, and the South Dakota Governor's Award. Jayne received top honors at the regional Professional Photographers of America annual awards ceremony in Brainerd, Minnesota, and one of her photos went on to score third place in the National Gallery Elite competition. In March 2003, Jayne was named the "South Dakota Photographer of the Year."

Jayne has been the guest speaker for numerous clubs and schools and has served as a mentor for the Homeless Children's Photography Project. She actively displays her work, most recently at the Sioux Falls Community Playhouse, Civic Fine Arts Center, Plains Museum, and Deerfield Bank.

MARK KAYSER

Mark Kayser is a native to South Dakota and has been photographing and writing about the outdoors since junior high. His photography has earned him numerous honors including first place awards from the National Travel and Tourism Association and the Outdoor Writers Association of America.

Mark is a columnist for *North American Hunter, Bow Hunt America Magazine*, and the central states editor for *Cabela's Outfitter Journal*. His work has been published in nearly every major outdoor publication on the market today including *Field & Stream, Outdoor Life*, and *American Hunter*. In addition, his photographs have been on the cover of six books and several videos.

Besides outdoor photography and writing, Mark is an avid hunter with a special interest in big game. Currently, Mark co-hosts "North American Outdoors" on ESPN2 and "Outdoor Tales" on The Outdoor Channel.

GREG LATZA

Greg Latza has been a photojournalist in South Dakota since 1994. He received his degree in journalism and geography from South Dakota State University. After a photojournalism internship with the *Milwaukee Journal* and a photojournalism position at the *Salina Journal*, Greg worked for the Sioux Falls *Argus Leader* for three years before starting Peoplescapes, a freelance photography and publishing business. Greg's wife Jodi works with him as a writer and graphic designer for Peoplescapes. They have two children, Anna and Luke.

The bulk of Greg's work is editorial photojournalism, including assignment work for the *New York Times, USA Today, Washington Post*, and the *Associated Press*. His magazine clients include *Farm Journal, Farm and Ranch Living*, and *South Dakota Magazine*.

The Latza's have four books to their credit: *Back on the Farm*, documenting South Dakota's farms and ranches; *South Dakota: An Alphabetical Scrapbook*, a children's book written by Jodi with photographs by Greg; *Hometown S.D., Life in Our Small Towns*, which offers a glimpse of life in more than 100 small towns across South Dakota; and *The Missouri*, with stories by Kevin Woster and photographs by Greg, about the Missouri River within South Dakota.

JOHNNY SUNDBY

Johnny Sundby photographs western South Dakota and eastern Wyoming. He works as a freelance photographer and has been published in numerous magazines, including *Family Circle, Field and Stream, Forbes, Golf Digest, People, Runner's World*, and *Time*. He has also been published in such newspapers as the *Chicago Tribune, Denver Post, Los Angeles Times, New York Times*, and *USA Today*.

Johnny's first book, *In God's Country, Photographs of the Black Hills and Badlands*, has sold more than 27,000 copies. In 1995, Johnny was named "Best Photographer in South Dakota" by *Eyes on You* magazine. Johnny has also won several awards for this work in the *Rapid City Journal*.

Johnny enjoys capturing landscapes and people of the West and especially cowboy and American Indian culture.

Index

Index

Index

Index

Index

Dining Dakota Style

The Junior League of Sioux Falls, Inc.
P.O. Box 85433
Sioux Falls, SD 57118-5433
Phone: (605) 336-9469
Web site: jlsiouxfalls.org
E-mail: info@jlsiouxfalls.org

Ordering Instructions: Complete this form and mail to the address above
or visit our Web site.

YOUR ORDER	QTY	TOTAL
Dining Dakota Style at $22.95 per book		$
Shipping and handling at $4.00 for one book; $3.00 for each additional book		$
	Subtotal	$
South Dakota residents add 6% sales tax to Subtotal (No tax if mailing outside the state of South Dakota)	Tax	$
	TOTAL	$

Ship To: *(Please print. If multiple Ship To Addresses, please attach to the form.)*

Name

Street Address

City   State   Zip

Telephone   E-mail

Method of Payment: [ ] Check made payable to Junior League of Sioux Falls
                            [ ] VISA   [ ] MasterCard   [ ] Discover

Name *(Print as it appears on the card.)*

Account Number   Expiration Date

Last 3 or 4 digits on back of card *(required for processing)*

Cardholder's Signature

Junior League Of Sioux Falls
Women Building a Stronger Community

Photocopies will be accepted.

Cookbook sale proceeds benefit the many community projects of the Junior League of Sioux Falls.